ALSO BY JEN MANN

Just a Few People I Want to Punch in the Throat: Volumes 1-6

How I F*cking Did It: From Moving Elves on Shelves to Making Over Six-Figures on the Internet and You Can Too

My Lame Life: Queen of the Misfits

Working with People I Want to Punch in the Throat: Cantankerous Clients, Micromanaging Minions, and Other Supercilious Scourges

People I Want to Punch in the Throat: Competitive Crafters, Drop Off Despots, and Other Suburban Scourges

Spending the Holidays with People I Want to Punch in the Throat

I Just Want to Hang Out With You

Will Work for Apples

You Do You!

But Did You Die?

I Just Want to Be Perfect

I STILL Just Want to Pee Alone

I Just Want to Be Alone

I Just Want to Pee Alone

TRAVELING WITH PEOPLE I WANT TO PUNCH IN THE THROAT

TRAVELING WITH PEOPLE I WANT TO PUNCH IN THE THROAT

BAREFOOT PASSENGERS, ARMREST
HOGGERS, AND OTHER TRAVELING
TROUBLEMAKERS

JEN MANN

THROAT PUNCH MEDIA, LLC

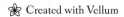 Created with Vellum

AUTHOR'S NOTE

All of the names and identifying characteristics of the people who appear in this book have been changed to protect the good, the bad, and the ugly. So if you think you can see yourself in these pages, please be assured that you are almost certainly wrong. These are my stories and this is how I remember them.

CAST OF CHARACTERS

Jen: Me. Unless you know me from pre-1990, in which case I'm Jenni. Notice, it's not "Jennifer." My parents didn't name me Jennifer. That would have been too trendy. They wanted to be original when naming me the most popular name of the decade. Instead they went wild and put their own flavor on a classic by putting an "i" on the end, thereby killing all possibility of me becoming a heart surgeon. Think about it, who would you trust more to do your bypass: Dr. Mandi or Dr. Amanda? When you have a name that ends in an adorable "i" that can only be written with a heart for a dot, it guarantees you'll end up on either the pole or the keyboard. Luckily, I chose the keyboard. I'm sarcastic, grumpy, and sweary. You've been warned.

The Hubs: I'm married to Ebeneezer, but I usually call him the Hubs. You can call him the Hubs too. Everyone does. He's used to it. He's Chinese and I'm Caucasian, sometimes that's helpful to know. He's a cheap bastard who can be a tad antisocial and a bit of a know-it-all, but he treats me like gold, so he's my lobster. The foundation of our marriage is built on relentless teasing of one another, constant griping, and the knowledge that no one else could stand us, so we'd better make this work. Oh yeah, I forgot about love. I meant to say love is the foundation of our marriage—the love of bickering.

Gomer and Adolpha (aged sixteen and fourteen at the writing of this book): Before you have a hissy fit and sit down to write me a nasty letter about my children's horrible names, just stop. *Of course* those aren't their real names. Come on. Do you think I'm an idiot? Their real names are actually worse, but I can't take the ridicule so I just made up what I consider to be horrific names for them. I get the most hate mail about their names. Why? Because people can't read.

Stan the Mann: Our dog.

My Dad: My dad has one of those old school jobs where he has to meet his clients in person. (Zoom is a dirty word to him.) So, every week he's winging around the planet so he can put on a suit and shake hands with mucky mucks in actual board rooms. Because of all this travel, he is kind of a big wig on a certain airline. Like the pilot always personally thanks him for flying and shit. It's weird but I don't complain when it means I get to use his frequent flier miles to travel.

My Mom: For most of my childhood my mom was a stay-at-home mom. She is a classic overachiever who treats shopping, decorating, and housekeeping like full-time high-paying jobs. Once my brother and I moved out, she started tagging along with my dad on his business trips when he went somewhere "interesting" and she's a top-tier frequent flier in her own right.

C.B.: My younger, smarter brother. Also a fake name. In fact, you can just assume that every name you read in this book besides Jen or Jenni is not real. C.B. has an important "real" job in the outside world and he is a little concerned that his boss might read this book. (As if his boss reads anything but *Robb Report* and *Yachting Magazine*!) Anyway, C.B. would like to remain as anonymous as possible just in case he decides to run for president someday or join a country club. He's married to Ida and they have two kids, Sherman and Violet.

ONE

PEOPLE I WANT TO PUNCH IN THE THROAT PUNCH LIST:

THE INTERMODAL TOUR EDITION

"The gentle reader will never, never know what a consummate ass he can become until he goes abroad." - Mark Twain

---

Packing. No matter how many lists I make or how many times I double-check everyone's suitcase, someone always leaves their underwear at home.

Laundry. There is something about traveling that makes my laundry disgusting and double in size.

Exhaustion. I need a vacation after my vacation—especially once I do all that gross laundry.

Other travelers. Seriously. I don't know who I hate

more: the woman who took off her shoes on the airplane or the guy who sat next to me in the gate area and watched porn. Some of you assholes should never leave your houses.

Sleeping in an unknown bed. Personally, I love a good hotel bed, but my family can't seem to settle down that first night on the road. It's like living in the *Princess and the Pea* times three.

Pooping in an unknown bathroom. I have no trouble doing my business on the road and with an audience outside the door, but my kids treat a hotel bathroom like it's sacred ground. "I need privacy, please. Can everyone go down to the lobby while I poop?"

Not pooping at all. The Hubs has "nervous bowels" that only like to vacate in the comfort of his home throne. It's a whole thing when he finally poops on vacation.

The signs that say "50 miles to the next rest area." I might have no trouble popping a squat just about anywhere, but I am a woman of a certain age, so I have trouble holding my bladder. I've learned that fifty miles is too damn far to hold back the floodgates.

Kids complaining they're bored. Spoiler alert: kids are just as bored at the beach or in the mountains as they are at home. Why do we even bring them with us?

Airline fees. You find a fare for $89 and read the small print to discover that price doesn't include a seat to sit in. When you call to inquire, the customer service representative says, "Oh you wanted a seat? That's a hundred bucks more. With a seat-belt is two-fifty. The FAA requires you to have a seat and a seat-belt. We also need to charge you for your wallet. That counts as a carry-on. Thank you for flying these amazing skies!"

The time change. Sometimes the time change will fuck you up. One time I went to Asia and took my birth control at the wrong time and got pregnant. (Don't worry, Gomer, we totally wanted you! Just not right then...)

The weather. You can check all the 10-day forecasts out there and still not pack correctly.

TSA pat downs. One day I was on my way to a book-signing when a TSA agent pulled me out of line to check cleavage for a weapon (the underwire in my bras always set off the metal detectors). Another TSA agent was carefully opening my suitcase to reveal a stack of books that resembled a bomb on the x-ray machine's monitor. The agent with my suitcase looked confused when she saw the title of the books. *"People I Want to Punch in the Throat,"* she read. She called to her co-worker, "Hey, Janet, be careful with that one. She *really* likes this book!"

First-time travelers in the security line. You can always spot the newbs. They're the ones carrying a full coffee cup and their liquids are at the very bottom of their carry-on bag. After they chug their hot coffee because it's airport coffee that cost $10, dig out their damn toiletries and find out their hairspray can is too large and needs to be thrown out, they always get flagged for change in their pockets. When I'm stuck behind them all I can think is, *Who the fuck still carries change in their pockets?*

The hotel website pictures never match the room. I would like to speak to the manager, please, because this is not what I expected. Not. At. All.

That one guy who hops up while the plane is still taxiing to the gate. We get it, sir. You're incredibly important and you have somewhere to be. Don't mind us, we're all just flying to Cleveland for fun. You're an asshole and we all hope when you open the overhead bin, a bag falls on your head.

The kid who kicks the back of my seat. I'm a mom. I get it. Traveling with kids is hard. But so help me god, if your kid kicks the back of my seat one more time I'm going to punch YOU in the throat. Also, put some fucking headphones on him, no one wants to listen to "Paw Patrol."

Anyone who reclines their seat. I said what I said. There's not enough leg room for that shit.

TWO

BERETS DON'T LOOK GOOD ON ANYONE, AND OTHER LIES I TOLD MY MIDDLE-SCHOOL SELF

PARIS, FRANCE

1984

If you asked me to list my favorite cities in the world, Paris would near the top. I've loved Paris since the first time I visited at 12 years old.

I love the architecture. I love the Seine. I love the outdoor bistros, shopping, and art. But, if I'm being honest, I mostly love anything chocolate. And the croissants.

When I think back to my first time in Paris, food was a very important part of that trip. We stayed in a hotel where they'd feed us breakfast in the lobby every morning. It wasn't an American-style buffet like at a Best Western. It was a very French breakfast. Everyone was served a hard roll and croissant with a pot of freshly brewed tea—unless you were a 12-year-old kid and her little brother.

As soon as we were seated at our table, the waiter said, "*Bonjour*, children. Do you like *chocolat*?"

I was just learning French in school, so I felt incredibly worldly when I replied, "*Mais oui!*"

He smiled. "*Magnifique!*" he said, turning and rushing back to the kitchen.

I wasn't far enough along in my studies to know what he

said, but I felt fairly confident we were going to get a piece of chocolate. "He's getting us a candy bar," I whispered to my brother, C.B.

A few minutes later, the waiter returned with a gleaming silver tray that held a steaming pot and two small teacups. He placed the teacups in front of me and C.B. with a flourish. He picked up the pot and began pouring from nearly a foot above the cups. *"Et voila!"* he said, as the dark brown fluid flowed from the spout into our cups.

C.B. and I literally gasped. "Oh," I said. "It's hot chocolate!"

"Parisian hot chocolate," the waiter corrected me. "The best in the world!"

That was a high bar to set, but his hot chocolate cleared it easily. I can still remember my first sip and nothing in my life (excluding the occasional orgasm) has come close to the absolute pleasure and delicious satisfaction I felt that day.

Every morning my brother and I would savor our little pot of hot chocolate and fight over who got the last drops. If our mom had allowed us to lick the pot, we would have.

My parents took us on a lot of trips when we were younger, and to afford these trips, they had to cut costs somewhere. Paris was no different. We flew on frequent flyer points and stayed at a budget hotel with free (delicious) breakfast. We walked everywhere to save on metro fees. We hit all the free tourist sites and ate lunch from local markets.

We were about halfway through our trip before we even set foot in a restaurant, and it was only because of my friend, Sylvie. Sylvie was in my sixth-grade class and her grandmother, Brigitte, lived in Paris. When Brigitte heard we were coming to visit, she insisted on taking us out for lunch and a day of sightseeing. To this day, I have never met anyone like Brigitte.

I was a short, stumpy little girl with a terrible perm and braces. I felt incredibly boring and dowdy in Paris so I bought a beret hoping I'd look chic. Instead I looked ridiculous. I had just convinced myself that everyone looked ridiculous in berets, but then in walked Brigitte with a charming beret perched on her luxurious head of hair. She looked fucking fabulous in that damn beret! But it wasn't just the beret. Everything about Brigitte was fucking fabulous.

I knew she was Sylvie's grandmother, but my grandmothers were nothing like her! My grandmothers wore polyester pants and sensible shoes. Brigitte wore a silk dress and sky-high heels that showcased her amazeballs legs. And don't even get me started on the scarf thrown jauntily around her neck, tousled and flowing beautifully in the breeze but somehow never flying away. Brigitte's flawless face was unwrinkled, her makeup impeccable. I didn't even know a 50-year-old woman could look fucking fabulous before I met Brigitte.

When I saw Brigitte's outfit, I was positive we'd misunderstood what she had planned for the day. "I thought we're going to the Louvre," I whispered to my mom. "I want to see the *Mona Lisa*."

"I thought so, too," Mom whispered back.

"Where are her sneakers?" I asked. It was a long walk to the museum and my feet hurt walking the streets of Paris in Nikes. I couldn't imagine walking in hooker heels.

Brigitte couldn't speak a word of English and the only French my family knew was what I'd learned from six weeks of Intro French. I could barely ask for directions to the closest library or bathroom. So we couldn't communicate very well. Brigitte just kept smiling at us and saying, *"D'accord."* After a bit of charades, we discovered that

Brigitte had a car parked nearby and she was going to drive us to the museum.

We piled into her tiny Renault and I clutched my mom's hand when Brigitte rolled down her window and made a little wave, pulling out into the busy traffic without so much as a glance in any mirror. She drove with her foot firmly on the gas, no hands on the wheel, and her head on a swivel, talking animatedly and pointing out various things along the way. Because we couldn't understand a word of what she was saying, we all just smiled and nodded.

"Ooh...ahh..." we said, over and over again without a clue as to what we were looking at. For all we knew, Brigitte could have been showing us a palace or her podiatrist's office. I was utterly and completely lost until we turned a corner and I could see a familiar landmark ahead.

"That's the Arc de Triomphe," I whispered to my mom. "Madame Carson has a poster of it on the wall in her classroom."

"Wow," Mom said. "It's impressive. I wonder if we'll get any closer."

It was as if Brigitte could understand Mom, because she headed straight for the Arc de Triomphe and the insane roundabout that circles it.

As we approached the monument, Brigitte announced proudly, "Arc de Triomphe!"

"*Oui,*" I said, trying out my French on her.

Brigitte swung her head around and exclaimed, "*Oui! En Francais! Bien!*"

My dad, who was in the front seat, squirmed. "Brigitte," he said as we gained quickly on the bumper of the car in front of us. "Uh, the road...uh..."

Brigitte finally turned her attention to the car in front of us and rather than hitting the brakes, she jerked the wheel hard and avoided hitting them with millimeters to spare.

"Oh, my!" Mom exclaimed, grabbing me and C.B. "Hold on."

Brigitte maneuvered her car seamlessly and suddenly we were in the thick of the roundabout. Cars, trucks, and scooters swirled around the monument in what appeared to be a *very* dangerous dance. Horns honked as Brigitte effortlessly slid her car into impossibly small slots in the traffic. Dad kept mashing on an invisible brake and gripped the "oh shit" handle on the ceiling. Brigitte laughed and continued to navigate her car around the circle. Finally we came around a bend and stopped completely, but I could see that we were still in the roundabout. Dozens of vehicles streamed across the road in front of us. Dad was the first to realize what Brigitte had planned. "Brigitte, are we going *straight across?*" he asked, pointing frantically.

Brigitte nodded, determined. *"Oui,"* she said, gripping the steering wheel tight.

"Oh my god," Dad said. "We're going to cross all these lanes to exit the roundabout."

"Where's the light?" Mom asked, looking around.

Dad turned around and stared Mom in the eye. "There is no light. From what I can tell, you just go when there's an opening."

"But there's never an opening," Mom said, fearfully eyeing the cross-traffic.

"Brigitte," Dad said. "Shouldn't we go around again? Get to the edge?" He motioned with his hand to show her what he meant.

Brigitte shook her head emphatically. *"Non,"* she said, tapping her watch. Clearly, Brigitte was on a schedule and hot-lapping the Arc de Triomphe three or four times to merge properly and exit wasn't part of her plan.

Suddenly Brigitte spotted a break in the sea of vehicles the rest of us couldn't see. Her shoulders tensed and she announced, *"Allons y!"*, stomped the gas pedal, and we were off. I felt my mother tighten her grip on my arm and saw her fling an arm in front of C.B. like a makeshift seat-belt. I closed my eyes and prayed I wouldn't die in Paris. *But if you're going to die somewhere cool,* I thought. *Paris wouldn't be so bad. My friends will be so jealous!*

I might have passed out at that point, because I don't remember anything between the roundabout and lunch at a fancy ass restaurant on the Champs-Elysees. Let me just say that of course I don't remember the museum, but I do recall the chocolate mousse. Sigh. I told you my favorite memories of Paris revolve around food. Obviously there wasn't a creperie at the Louvre or I would have remembered my first glimpse of the famous *Mona Lisa.*

We knew Brigitte was going to take us to her favorite restaurant in all of Paris. When we made our initial plans, Sylvie's mother had explained, "When you are in Paris, you must eat the best food and my mother will make sure you're well taken care of. She insists."

Once Dad glanced at the prices on the menu and deter-mined lunch would cost more than our entire hotel stay, he whispered, "You'll eat whatever Brigitte orders and you'll smile and say *gracias.*"

"It's *merci,*" I whispered back.

"You know what he means," Mom hissed. "The prices at this restaurant are astronomical. Do *not* embarrass us."

Ironically, it was Mom who almost embarrassed our family. You see, my parents are teetotalers. The rumor is Dad used to drink "the occasional beer" back before he married Mom, the preacher's daughter. After that, he quit cold turkey. Until that lunch with Brigitte, I don't think alcohol had ever touched Mom's lips. But we were in Paris. The land of Burgundy and Bordeaux. There was no way Brigitte was going to eat her escargot without a delicious chardonnay!

When the enormous bottle of wine arrived at the table, Mom's eyes got big as dinner plates. Mom never cusses, but her face said, *Oh, shit. Not today, Satan.*

She smiled brightly and said, "No, *merci.*" She placed a hand over her wine glass.

"*Non?*" the waiter asked, aghast.

"*Non?*" Brigitte asked, equally aghast.

Dad was rattled. "Um, you see, um, my wife...she...no drinks wine." He grimaced and shook his head.

Brigitte frowned for half a second and then her eyes lit up. "Ah!" she said, nodding. She turned to the waiter and rattled off a slew of commands.

He nodded and turned back to the bar with the bottle still in hand.

Dad nodded gratefully. "*Merci,*" he said. "No wine."

Brigitte smiled broadly. "No wine," she agreed.

Two minutes later the waiter returned with an even bigger bottle of champagne. Without waiting for any complaints, the waiter popped the cork with dramatics I'd only ever seen in a movie.

Brigitte clapped her hands excitedly and said, "Celebrate, *oui?*"

"Ahh," Mom said, plastering a fake smile on her face. "Champagne?"

"Expensive French champagne. Drink it," Dad growled.

"Don't embarrass us," I said, gleefully.

That lunch was *incroyable* because it was the first (and

only) time I've ever seen my mom tipsy. She's a fun drunk, y'all. She was giggly and talkative and silly. I would argue it was a good thing, because she needed to be a little hammered when it came time to eat the escargot.

Luckily, C.B. and I got passes. I had just steeled myself to reach for a slimy snail when the waiter presented me with a plate containing a sizzling steak and...

"French fries!" C.B. exclaimed. "French fries in France!"

And then, to top it off, Brigitte ordered chocolate mousse for dessert.

Now, my brain is foggy and I have a tendency to embellish my memories, especially when I'm thinking back to over thirty-five years ago, but I swear the chocolate mousse was served in an enormous crystal vase and rolled out on a cart. It was like something out of *Willy Wonka*. The waiter scooped out generous portions of the fluffy dessert into silver bowls. Every time C.B. and I emptied a bowl, the waiter would immediately refill it. I had no idea if Brigitte bought the whole vat of mousse or paying by the scoop, but I just kept eating. I didn't want to be rude.

Finally, Mom was drunk on champagne and C.B. and I were drunk on chocolate mousse, so it was time for Brigitte to take us back to our hotel. We were making our way to Brigitte's car when we came to a large avenue we needed to cross. I could see a crosswalk further down the street, but Brigitte's car was directly across from us. Brigitte had no intention of going out of her way to cross the street (plus, with those heels, I figured she needed to take as few steps as possible). So, she hiked up the hem of her dress a bit to show off more of her shapely leg and stepped out into the street. "*Arrêtez!*" she cried, holding up her hand to the oncoming traffic.

There were probably five or six lanes of traffic and every single car came to a stop. One man even lowered his window and yelled at Brigitte. But he wasn't mad. My French wasn't good enough to know what he said exactly, but I could understand he was letting Brigitte know that he'd stop for her any time she'd like. Brigitte stood in the middle of the road like a crossing guard and shooed us all across. I was enthralled by Brigitte and her powerful ways.

For the rest of the trip, I couldn't stop thinking about Brigitte. I wanted to have that kind of power over cars and men and waiters and food and scarves and berets. I wanted to be interesting and stunning well into my fifties. I wanted to live in Paris and wear five-inch heels and berets. I was so jealous of Sylvie. She had Brigitte's DNA. She actually had a chance for all that shit to come true!

I decided it wasn't just genes, though: It was attitude. I needed to adopt Brigitte's *no fucks given* attitude. I needed to trust in my feminine wiles to get what I wanted. And I needed to just believe I was as glamorous as Brigitte. Mind over matter and all that shit.

I decided to test out my theory one afternoon when I stuck out my ham-like leg, stepped confidently off the curb, and yelled, "*Arrêtez!*"

I heard my mother scream, "Jenni!" but I was already committed. I was alluring and intoxicating like Brigitte. I just needed to *believe* it. *I believe the cars will stop,* I thought. *They will stop!*

Only the cars did not stop. It was like a cartoon where the cars all swerve and barely miss one another to avoid the idiot in the road. Cars and trunks honked at me and drivers cursed me in French and English. I think I even heard German once.

Dad reached out and snatched me back onto the sidewalk. "What were you thinking?" he yelled.

"I thought they'd stop. They stopped for Brigitte." I was practically in tears.

C.B. snorted. "Yeah because Brigitte is hot," he said.

I learned that day that no amount of confidence or berets could stop oncoming traffic if you were a doughy middle-school girl.

On our last night in Paris I almost died again. We'd gone to a nearby pizzeria for dinner. After a week in Paris, my dad decided that was the night he would finally try to speak French. He'd noticed that when we ordered four Coca-Colas the servers would always repeat, *"Quatre cocas."* He'd been on us to try and fit in better in Paris. "You look like ugly Americans when you're speaking English all the time," he'd said.

Meanwhile, he was the one always asking, "English? Speak English?" but whatever.

For some reason, maybe it was because it was our last night in Paris or maybe because the pizzeria was completely empty so there was no one to laugh at him, he tried his French. He ordered a pepperoni pizza by pointing at a picture on the wall and then said, *"Et quatre cocas."*

The man behind the counter looked at all us closely and repeated, *"Quatre cocas?"*

"Oui," Dad said, beaming.

"Quatre??" the man confirmed.

"Oui," Dad said.

"Un, deux, trois, quatre," the man counted, pointing at each one of us.

"Oui," Dad said. *"Quatre."*

The man shrugged and said, "Okay."

A bit later he and a teenage boy emerged from the kitchen and brought five pizzas to our table.

"Um..." Dad said, quizzically.

"Un pepperoni et quatre cocas," the man said.

"Um..."

The man spoke to the boy in rapid French.

"My father and I think there is a problem, sir?" The boy spoke English with a heavy French accent.

"Yes," Dad replied. "We ordered a pepperoni pizza."

"Yes, this is here," the boy said, motioning to the round pepperoni pizza. "And four *coca* pizzas."

"Four what?" Dad exclaimed.

"*Coca* pizzas." He pointed to the square pizzas. "My father thought it was too many but you insisted, sir."

"There's a pizza called coca?" Mom asked.

"Yes, it is just here. The Spanish pizza," the boy said, indicating the additional pizzas.

Mom grabbed a menu and scanned it. She found what she was looking for and pointed it out to Dad.

Realization dawned on Dad's face and he turned bright red with embarrassment. "Oh, no. I meant four *Coca-Colas*," Dad said.

We were still the only diners in the pizzeria, the room went quiet as everyone understood the miscommunication. I held my breath and stared at the owner. He was a large man who had not smiled once since we'd arrived. I was worried that we couldn't pay for all that pizza. We'd specifically chosen the pizzeria for dinner because Dad was low on francs. (Remember, this was the 1980s so credit cards weren't as prevalent as they are now. If you didn't have francs or Traveler's Checks, you were S.O.L.) "Are we going to French jail?" I whispered to Mom.

"Shh," she said, patting my leg under the table. "It's

okay. I have dollars." She seemed calm, but I could feel the tension in the room as she and Dad waited to see how this man would react to our blunder.

Finally, a huge smile spread across the man's face and he shook with laughter. "Coca-Colas?" he exclaimed. "Coca-Colas?"

His son nodded and laughed along with him.

"*Quatre Coca-Colas?*" The man practically screamed with laughter and he patted Dad heartily on the back. Dad winced but smiled hopefully.

"*Oui, Papa,*" the boy said. The father and son spoke to one another quickly in French and the man took off toward the kitchen. The boy turned to us. "My father will now get you the Coca-Colas."

"No!" we all exclaimed in unison.

The boy was surprised. "But I thought that is what you ordered."

Dad stood up and said, "Yes, I tried to order that but I made a terrible mistake. I don't need the Coca-Colas now. I just have barely enough to pay for these extra pizzas. I can't afford drinks too."

"Ah. Okay," the boy said. He returned to the kitchen leaving us sitting there, dazed and confused about what had transpired.

"I should have let Jenni order," Dad muttered.

I frowned. Yeah, right! I would have made the same mistake and we would not all be laughing about it right now. I would be washing dishes in the back to pay off my debt.

The door to the kitchen opened and the owner and his son returned carrying four ice cold bottles of Coca-Cola. "*Et, voila,*" he said, placing a bottle in front of each of us.

"No, please," Dad said. "I explained to your son—"

The boy cut him off. "My father says he's never laughed so hard. The Coca-Colas are his thanks to you."

"But what about the pizza?" Dad asked. "It's too much food. Can someone here eat it?"

The boy whistled loudly and two of the biggest mastiffs I've ever seen (before or since) emerged from the kitchen. They came over and sat obediently at his feet. One dog was right beside me and his enormous head towered over mine. I could see a thin line of drool dripping from its mouth and I could feel the heat radiating from its large body. It yawned widely and I was amazed by the size of its razor-sharp teeth. I had a friend whose family owned a jewelry store and they kept Doberman Pinchers for security. They raised the dogs in their home and the dogs were obedient and gentle with family members but ruthless to intruders. We had a sleep-over and the girl went to get us some popcorn, leaving me alone with one of the Dobermans. While the girl was in the room, the dog had been docile and friendly, but as soon as she left, something changed in the dog. Immediately her eyes went dark and she raised up from the floor with a low growl. I was immobilized with fear. The dog advanced on me but before she got too close, the girl's mother burst into the room and shouted commands at the dog. The dog immediately calmed down and backed off. The mother explained the dog wasn't bad; she was "just doing her job." She was a guard dog and I was a stranger, and "there are no bad dogs only bad owners." The two mastiffs reminded me of the Doberman Pinchers. They were clearly there for security and they were calm and docile now but with one word they could eat me and C.B. like a snack. I hoped they had good owners. I felt a little sick.

"I can pay for it," Dad said, his worried eyes darted between the two giant dogs.

"Is okay," the boys assured him. He picked up a coca pizza and flung it like a Frisbee into the corner of the room. The dogs' ravenous eyes watched the pizza fly through the air and land with a thud on the tile floor, but they didn't move. The boy picked up a second coca pizza and flung it into another corner of the room. Again, the dogs watched, but never twitched a muscle. Until—the boy uttered a quiet order—and they were off! The dogs separated and each one attacked their own coca pizza. Within mere seconds the pizzas were devoured, the floor licked clean.

I wanted my final memories of Paris to be food, so the next morning I savored every bite of my last croissant and nursed my hot chocolate until it was cold chocolate (still delicious by the way). I arrived back in the United States feeling five pounds heavier, but also worldly and interesting. Everyone else had gone to Florida for spring break and come back with sunburns. I was the only one who returned with a beret. It still looked like shit on me, but I believed it looked amazing and that was the important part.

THREE

THAT ONE TIME I WAS MISTAKEN FOR AN INTERNATIONAL SPY. AND NOT IN A COOL JAMES BOND WAY.

BUDAPEST, HUNGARY

1993

My university had partnerships with universities around the world and every year they sent delegations of students to visit our "sister schools." I was selected to join the group going to Sofia, Bulgaria for the summer.

In our first informational meeting, Dr. Hill, the professor in charge of the trip, announced we'd be traveling via Budapest, Hungary, where we'd need to spend the night. "It's the only way to get there," he said.

This news surprised me. My parents had just returned from Sofia a few months before and did not have to travel through Budapest. I raised my hand. "I don't think that's true," I said. "My parents were just there and didn't have to overnight at all."

Dr. Hill said, "Trust me. My wife is a travel agent. She says it's the only way. Also, you'll need to book your plane tickets through her. That way we can all travel together." He glanced at his wife, who was also at the meeting.

Undeterred, I said, "My mom is also a travel agent. She'll want to book my tickets. If you tell me when to be in Sofia, she'll get me there."

"Absolutely not!" Mrs. Hill said. "I will be doing all the bookings. The school has only authorized me. My husband and I are in charge of you students and you must do what we say!"

Dr. Hill nodded. "That's right. We'll be traveling together. It's the only way to make sure you all get there safely."

When I returned to my dorm that night, I called my mom. "They said we have to overnight in Budapest," I said.

"That's ridiculous," Mom said. I could hear her typing on her computer. "I'm looking right here and that's completely unnecessary. There's no reason to overnight, unless—" she stopped typing. "Jen, do you think they're planning their own personal excursion to Budapest after Sofia? That's the only thing that makes sense. They're routing you through Budapest because *the Hills* want to go to Budapest."

At the next informational meeting I found out Mom was absolutely correct. When the itineraries were handed out and we could see that we were going through Budapest (at an additional $700 each) I asked, "Dr. Hill, are you planning a vacation in Budapest? Is that why we're going through there?"

Dr. Hill squirmed a bit but Mrs. Hill had no shame. "Yes! My husband and I are staying for a week there. We've rented an apartment already."

"Hang on. What's happening?" Kyle asked.

"They've added about *seven hundred dollars* to the cost of our trip because they want to go to Budapest," I said.

"More than that," added Lisa. "Because we'll have to get a hotel room too!"

"No, we won't," I said. I looked Mrs. Hill right in her

eye. "You said we're your responsibility, remember? Imagine just dumping us at the airport in Budapest and asking us to fend for ourselves? A bunch of kids in a foreign country? Nope, we'll come with you. There are only eight of us. We'll sleep on the floor of your apartment for the night."

Mrs. Hill opened her mouth to argue, but Dr. Hill put a hand on her arm. "It's fine," he murmured.

AT THE END of the summer, it was time to fly home. The flight from Sofia to Budapest was only about an hour and we arrived in the middle of the day. I noticed that as soon as we deplaned, the Hills bolted for the baggage claim area. "They're trying to ditch us," I warned Kyle.

"Did he give you the address?" Kyle asked, picking up his pace.

"Nope. I've been asking him for days and he kept telling me he needed to ask Mrs. Hill," I said. "And then when I did, she said she wrote it down somewhere and needed to find it."

Lisa was hot on our trail. "Are they making a run for it?" she asked.

"We think so," I said.

Lisa looked scared. "I'm out of money. I planned on staying at their place tonight," she said.

"I know," I said. "Don't worry. I won't let the Hills ditch us."

We jogged down to the baggage claim area and I saw Dr. Hill pulling a suitcase off the carousel. Mrs. Hill was beside him throwing furtive glances over her shoulder.

"There's my bag," Kyle said. "I'll grab it and stay with them."

I saw my backpack slide down the chute behind Kyle's. "There's mine," I said. "Don't worry, Lisa. We're not going anywhere until the whole group is here."

I grabbed my bag and threw it over my shoulders, snapping all the straps into place as I walked over to Mrs. Hill. "Whoa, we almost lost you," I said.

Mrs. Hill frowned slightly. "We wanted to be first because we have so many bags," she said.

"Of course," I said. "Well, I think there are only five of us going with you. Kyle's got his bag and Lisa's over there waiting for hers. I think Jackie and Renee are in the bathroom, but they carried on their packs, so they're ready whenever you are."

"What do you mean you're going with us?" Dr. Hill asked.

I stared at him. "We're going to your apartment," I said. "We decided this months ago. At first I thought it would be all eight of us, but Oscar, Frank, and Jason are catching the Eurail to Poland or something, I think. I don't know. They're gone. But the rest of us are flying out tomorrow and we're staying at your place tonight."

"We don't have enough room," Mrs. Hill argued.

"We'll sleep on the floor. It's fine. My flight is at five o'clock in the morning. I'll be gone in the middle of the night."

"Well, then maybe you want to stay here, then?" Mrs. Hill said. "I hear cab fare is very expensive."

"No, that doesn't seem safe," I said. "The college wouldn't like it if something happened to us because we stayed overnight at the airport. It's fine. We'll just crash at your place."

I could see Jackie and Renee staking out the exit and Kyle was helping Lisa with her suitcase.

"We're all ready," I said. "Here, let me take this bag." I took Mrs. Hill's carry-on.

"That has the address in it!" she exclaimed.

"Oh, perfect!" I said, handing the bag back to her. "Let me write it down. We won't all fit in one cab."

"You can just follow us," Dr. Hill said.

I smiled but inside I was furious. "That's crazy. This is a very busy city. There's no way we can keep up. Just give me the address."

"I don't have a pen," Mrs. Hill said, weakly.

I was a fucking English major. I was more than prepared. I dug in one of the outside pockets of my backpack and came up with an assortment of pens, pencils, and notebooks. "Here you go," I said.

She scribbled an address on a notebook and handed it back to me.

"Thanks," I said, sweetly.

When we got outside, we hailed two cabs. The Hills were throwing their shit in the trunk of the first cab with wild abandon. "Do you think they gave us the right address?" Kyle whispered.

"Oh, shit," I said. I hadn't even thought of that. Surely they weren't that cold-hearted and/or stupid.

Jackie and Renee had overheard Kyle. Without a word, they slipped into the backseat of the Hill's cab. I didn't blame them. It was every man for himself at that point. The Hills had turned us against one another.

"Well, if the address is wrong at least we're all together, right?" Lisa said, hopefully.

"Of course," said Kyle.

The Hill's cab sped away from the curb and we hopped into ours. "Here's the address," I said, handing the driver the piece of paper. "But please follow that cab. We want to go the same way they're going."

He nodded and stomped the gas pedal.

We stayed close to the other cab and arrived about a half an hour later at the address Mrs. Hill had given me. "She didn't lie," I said.

"Good," said Lisa. "Because I was about ready to get Dr. Hill fired if they did."

Mrs. Hill also didn't lie about how small their apartment was. They'd rented a 500-square-foot studio apartment with a loft. She and Dr. Hill took the loft and let us flop on the couch and floor below.

I also didn't lie when I said I wouldn't be there long and I'd be leaving in the middle of the night. I caught a cab before dawn and headed to the airport to catch my flight home.

When I arrived at the airport, I checked my bag and cleared passport control. I had been sitting in my gate area for about an hour listening to my Walkman when I heard my name announced on the overhead speaker. Up until that point, all of the announcements had been a woman's voice speaking Hungarian followed by an English translation. This one was a man's voice and just in English. "Jenni Mann, please report to passport control. Jenni Mann to passport control."

I thought maybe I'd accidentally left my passport earlier, but when I checked my bag I could see it was still stuffed snug in a pocket.

I packed up my belongings and made my way back to passport control. As I drew closer, I could see two armed guards and a dog in my path. One held up a hand, indicating for me to stop. "Jenni Mann?" he asked.

The other guard looked at a paper in his hand and nodded. I could see the paper was a photocopy of my passport.

"Yes," I said, nervously.

"Come with us, please," the guard said. I was escorted into an off-limits area. "Leave your bag here."

I left my backpack with the other guard and the dog. The dog immediately began sniffing.

I was taken to a small interrogation room and the door was closed behind us.

"Sit, please." The guard motioned to a chair at the table.

I sat, utterly confused. "Can you tell me what's going on?" I asked.

"Wait here, please." He left me alone. I could see a camera was on me and I figured someone was watching. I didn't know what to do with myself. I sat there and fidgeted and probably looked guilty as hell even though I had no idea why I'd been put there.

After what seemed like an eternity, the guard came back and sat down opposite me.

"You were flagged as a security risk," the guard said. "I have some questions for you."

"A security risk?" I asked, even more confused.

"Why are you in Budapest?" he asked.

"I had a layover," I said.

"You came from Sofia yesterday?" he asked.

"Yes."

"Why did you come here?"

"Because I had a layover," I repeated.

"There are many flights you could have chosen that don't have layovers. Why did you choose this one?"

I sighed. Because of the fucking Hills. "Because I'm on

an exchange program for my college and the professor booked the trip because *he* wants to vacation in Budapest. So we all had to fly here and spend the night."

"Write down the name of your college," he said, sliding a piece of paper and pen toward me.

I wrote on the paper and slid it back. "You will be in trouble if you're lying," he said.

"I'm not lying," I said.

"What did you do while you were in Budapest?"

"Nothing," I said. It was true. I was too tired once we arrived at the apartment and I knew I had an early flight. Plus, I was a little worried the Hills would "accidentally" lock us out if we went to dinner.

"What is my colleague going to find in your bag?" he asked.

Fucking hell. "Nothing," I said, thanking God that I wasn't the kind of person who carries anything illicit in my bag.

"We're pulling your checked bag, too," he said. "What will we find in there?"

"Nothing!"

"What did you do in Bulgaria?"

"I was part of an exchange program. I went to school. I traveled a bit."

"Where did you travel?" he asked.

"I don't remember the names of the towns," I said. "The university arranged a tour. I just got on the bus."

"Why are you in Budapest?" he asked again.

Oh my god. This guy was like a broken record. I was starting to get irritated and a bit worried. I wasn't worried I was going to disappear; I was worried I was going to miss my flight. I glanced at my watch and I knew they were probably boarding my plane. "I'm trying to get out of here," I said. "My plane leaves in thirty minutes."

"Wait here," he said. As if I could leave.

He left me alone again.

After a few minutes, he returned with my carry-on. "Is this your bag?" he asked.

"Yes," I said, hesitantly. The bag had been out of my possession for an hour by then. I'd seen way too many cop shows to know anything could be planted in there by now.

"Shall we go through it together?" he asked.

"Okay," I said. I didn't see that I had any choice. No one had told me my rights. I was in a foreign country and no one had a clue where I was.

He opened all the pockets and started dragging out my belongings. Books, papers, pens, and pencils were strewn across the table. My wallet was emptied and he inspected all of my money.

Did he want money? I wondered. *Was I supposed to bribe him?*

I was just about to offer him money to let me go when the other guard entered the room. He was carrying my Walkman and my camera. He had a Ziploc bag full of my used film.

"What did you take pictures of?" he demanded.

"Um, just stuff. I don't know. The school, my friends, mountains, the beach," I said.

"Did you take a picture of people without their permission?" he asked.

"I don't know. Maybe?" I said.

"What are you doing in Budapest?"

FUUUUCK. "Nothing!" I said. "In fact, I want to get out of here. I want to go home. I've been traveling for a long time and I'm ready to sleep in my own bed. I would not have come here if it wasn't for my stupid teacher. I swear. I didn't even want to come to Budapest!"

Both of the guards frowned.

Oh shit, I thought. I just offended them, didn't I?

"I will make it easy for you," a guard said, folding his hands on the table. "You never have to come back to Budapest again. In fact, I insist you never come back. You are a security risk. I don't know what you're up to, but I don't want you in my country a minute longer. We are holding your plane and I will escort you personally out of my city."

They shoved everything back into my backpack, except my electronics and film. They were kept in a sealed plastic bag that closely resembled an evidence bag. "You can have this back when you arrive in New York," the guard said.

They placed bright orange stickers on the plastic bag and my backpack that said, SECURITY RISK. CHECK BY HAND.

The guard wasn't lying. He didn't just escort me to my gate, he walked me right onto the plane and all the way to my seat. Every single person on that plane stopped and watched us proceed down the aisle. They saw the bright orange stickers and whispered to one another. I can only imagine what they thought of the little, round, 21-year-old terrorist in their midst.

I was fuming. All I could do was sit there and silently curse the Hills.

After I was seated and belted in, the guard handed the baggie of electronics to the closest flight attendant. "She cannot have these until she lands in New York," he said.

The flight attendant nodded and scurried off with my items.

The guard knelt down and looked at me sternly. "Jenni

Mann," he said. "You have been deemed a security risk. Never return to Hungary again!"

I have no idea if he really had the authority to ban me, but to this day, I'm still afraid to risk it. And to this day, I've never forgiven the Hills for routing me through fucking Budapest.

FOUR

PEACE, LOVE, AND MUD. SO MUCH MUD

WOODSTOCK, NEW YORK

1994

"Hey Jen," my dad said, casually. "My client gave me VIP tickets to some big music concert. Your mom and I have no desire to go, but I'll give you the tickets if you agree to take your brother with you."

"I don't know," I said. I was reluctant because my brother had just graduated from high school the month before. He was an 18-year-old child and I was a very mature 22-year-old woman, thank you very much. He would definitely get in the way and harsh my buzz. I couldn't babysit him! I decided it would all depend upon who was on stage. "Who's the performer?"

My dad smiled. "Name a band you like."

I shrugged. "I don't know. The Red Hot Chili Peppers."

"Yep, they'll be there. Who else do you like?"

I frowned. "The Cranberries."

Dad nodded. "Sure. You'll see them. Keep going."

"Um, Violent Femmes."

"Absolutely. All of them, plus my personal favorite: Bob Dylan."

"What? What are you even talking about? What kind of concert has this kind of line up?"

"I've got tickets to Woodstock."

"What?" I screamed.

Woodstock '94 was literally the only thing everyone was talking about that summer. It was all over the radio, television, and magazines. I lived in Kansas, though, and the concert was in upstate New York, so I didn't know anyone who was actually making the trek to see the show.

"You have two tickets to Woodstock?" I asked.

"Nope, I have four tickets to Woodstock. If you take your brother, you can each bring a friend too."

"How are we going to get there?" The concert was only a couple of weeks away and flights weren't cheap. Plus, there was nowhere to fly into that was very close.

"I figured you'd drive."

A road trip! I'd never been on a road trip that far before. I was in! I didn't care that I had to bring C.B. I would have agreed to take anyone.

If you remember way back to 1994 you'll remember that cellphones and GPS were not in wide use, so Dad took to me the local AAA storefront to get me some maps. "She's driving from here to Saugerties, New York," he told the woman assisting us.

"Well, then, let's get her there the fastest and safest route possible," she said, grabbing several maps and a bright yellow highlighter.

When she was done highlighting the entire route, showcasing the cleanest rest stops and alerting me to road work, she piled what felt like eleventy-billion maps into my arms and told me to have a great time at the concert.

. . .

THE CONCERT WAS SUPPOSED to last three days, so everyone needed to pack a tent. I didn't know anything about camping back then. (Ha. I wrote that like I've since learned more about camping in the past twenty-five years or something. Nope. I still don't know about camping.) I really didn't want to buy a tent, because when would I ever use it again? It would literally still be in my basement today if I'd bought one.

I'd offered my extra ticket to my friend, Osbert. He was the lucky winner for a few reasons: 1. He didn't have a job; 2. He was fun to hang out with; and 3. He didn't have a job (so many people said no because they couldn't get time off that fast).

Osbert ended up being the perfect choice, though. He knew about camping and took me to a local camping store so we could rent a tent.

"How big do you want?" the sales guy asked.

"Big," I said. "I'll want my own space." My brother was bringing a friend and I'd be crammed into a tent with three boy-men. I wanted some area to claim as my own.

"Well, not too big," Osbert said. "We have to fit it in the car, Jen. Along with everything else. And we're not living in it all day or anything. We're just sleeping there for three nights, or whatever. It doesn't need to be anything spectacular."

"It should have a window at least," I argued. "I'll want to air it out."

Osbert laughed. "Oh my god, Jen. It just needs a door. I promise, it will be fine. The budget is the most important thing here. We need something affordable."

The tent guy said, "I have the perfect one." He showed us a slightly battered orange four-person tent with a door and window, and within our budget.

"We'll take it," Osbert said.

Now, the thing to know about Osbert is that he was a very dear friend, but he never had money when it was important (see above where I told you he didn't have a job and thus, was available for a week-long road trip). That day was no exception. We needed a credit card to pay for the tent rental and we were asked to put a damage deposit down too. "I left my wallet at my apartment," Osbert said.

"How convenient," I replied.

"I'm good for it," Osbert promised.

I reluctantly handed over my credit card, but I was worried, because I was putting down a $400 deposit on a shitty tent. I was certain that after three boys spent a weekend in that tent, I'd never see my money again. *I should have just bought a tent,* I thought.

FINALLY THE DAY arrived to hit the road. Osbert and I loaded up my Jeep Cherokee and shoved C.B. and his friend, Roland, into the backseat. I had all the maps from AAA, but my dad was worried that wouldn't be enough, so he'd also typed up several pages of additional instructions. It was like he moonlighted for AAA or something!

Through one stretch of Missouri, Osbert read aloud, "There isn't much for the next eighty miles, so the next exit is a good place to refuel and get some snacks. You've got a long night ahead of you, so get something with caffeine."

In Illinois Dad warned us, "Tollbooth ahead, get in the far-right lane. Everyone gravitates left, so it will move faster. There is exact change in the ashtray."

And when we got to Indiana, Osbert read, "It's now midnight. Time to trade drivers, Jen. You've been driving too long. Take a nap and let C.B. drive because in a few hours you're going to be in Columbus traffic and you'll need to take over."

"Ha!" I exclaimed. "He's wrong! It's not midnight! It's only eleven!"

"Hang on," Osbert said, consulting the binder Dad had given us. "You've crossed into the eastern time zone, change your watches."

"Damn him!"

Over twenty hours later we finally pulled into Saugerties, New York. We followed the signs to a large field where we were directed to park. The VIP passes allowed us into the venue a day early so it wasn't very crowded yet. There were dozens of people milling about, but I couldn't see the stage anywhere. "What now?" I asked Osbert. "Is this it?"

A guy walking by stopped and said, "You gotta catch the bus to Winston Farm." He pointed out a line of people on the other side of the field.

"We carry everything from here?" Osbert asked.

The guy sort of frowned. "Everything? What else do you need besides a bowl?" He took off, shaking his head.

"A bowl?" I asked. "Is he going to make salad?"

Osbert burst out laughing. "Oh, Jen. This is going to be an eye-opening weekend for you."

"He's talking about drugs," Roland said. "You need a bowl to smoke pot."

"Shut up, Roland," I snapped. "I was making a joke." (I wasn't. I really thought they were making salad. Maybe soup. But I definitely wasn't thinking about pot.)

"Okay, everyone, grab your stuff," Osbert said. "And let's catch the bus." He threw the tent on his shoulder and once again I was grateful I'd invited him instead of some weak ass boy. And he was probably grateful he'd talked me out renting a bigger tent.

That first night was incredible. The place was practically empty. We could walk around and see all the stages. We had the pick of the place to pitch our tent. "Can we please put the tent near the toilets?" I asked, pointing out the row of port-a-potties on the hill above us. "I'll need to go in the night and I don't want to walk that far."

Osbert surveyed the land and shook his head. "I think that's a bad idea, Jen. What do you think it means when they say, 'shit rolls downhill?'"

"I don't know," I said. "I just don't want to be that far away."

"Yeah, but we also don't want to be that close," Osbert said. "Here's the thing, tonight this place is great, but tomorrow when the real concert starts, there's going to be a shitload of people coming in. I've been to enough of these kinds of thing to know things easily go wrong and we don't want to be camped at the bottom of that hill."

We ended up setting up our tent near the middle of the field. Our closest neighbors were a few yards away. We spread out a blanket that night and listened to live music until after midnight.

I went to bed that night so pleased with everything. We'd arrived safely and our tent was in a great spot to see the north stage perfectly. *It's going to be a great weekend*, I thought as I drifted off to sleep.

The next morning I was awakened by somebody falling into the outside wall of my tent and stepping on my head. "Ow!" I yelled.

Osbert was out the door in a flash. I heard him say, "What the fuck, man?"

"Fuck you, dude," someone replied.

I pulled on my shoes and scrambled outside to join Osbert. When I emerged from the tent, I almost ran straight into the back wall of another tent. Osbert grabbed me at the last second before I put my foot through it. I looked around us, stunned to see the transformation that had happened overnight. The gates had opened to the general ticket holders just after midnight and people had been streaming in since then, setting up their tents everywhere and anywhere. The several yards we'd enjoyed the night before between us and our nearest neighbors were now filled with dozens of tents. The guy who had stepped on my head was driving a tent stake into the ground. No, not into the ground, he was driving it into the fabric of our tent and *then* into the ground! "Hey," I said. "You're putting a hole in our tent!"

The guy looked up from what he was doing. "So what?"

"It's a rental," I said, weakly. "I'll be charged extra."

He laughed and walked away.

"Asshole," Osbert said.

"There's always one in every bunch," a voice said.

I turned and saw a man and woman putting up a small tent. It was the man who had spoken. He was as old as my parents and had stringy gray hair and a pot belly peeking out from under his tie-dyed t-shirt. He wore ratty shorts and flip flops. The lady with him had long frizzy gray hair down to the middle of her back. She wore a caftan and flip flops.

"It's too bad," the woman said, shaking her head sadly. "That's not the spirit of Woodstock."

"You guys are originals, aren't you?" Osbert asked.

I didn't need him to ask. I knew by looking at them.

The man laughed. "Originals? I like that better than 'old folks!'"

The woman nodded. "Someone on the bus called us old folks. It really pissed Barney off."

"Yeah, we're originals," Barney said. "Bev and I were

here for the first Woodstock and now we're here for this one."

"Well, we were here for the first one, but we didn't come together," Bev said. "I was dating Simon in those days."

Barney winked at me. "And where's Simon now?" he asked.

Bev giggled. "Who knows?"

"That's right, baby," Barney said.

Bev got kind of serious and pulled me aside. "Listen, it can get hairy this weekend. If you need any help, Barney and I are right here."

I was kind of taken aback. "Oh, I'll be fine," I said.

"You don't have to do anything you don't want to do," Bev said, sternly. She gave Osbert a dirty look.

But Osbert wasn't the problem. In fact, he was the one who protected me all weekend. Especially when Barney gave me trouble the next day.

The next morning I woke up to a steady rain. I stepped out of my tent and was immediately greeted by a soaking wet Barney wearing nothing but a g-string.

"Good morning, Jen!" Barney said, shaking his hips.

"Wow, where are your pants, Barney?" I asked.

"I lost them in the mosh pit," Barney said.

I looked around. "Where's Bev?"

"I lost her in the mosh pit, too."

"Gotcha," I said.

Osbert emerged from the tent carrying his camera. He hadn't packed clean underwear, but he'd packed loads of film. He immediately started snapping photos.

"Take a picture of me and your girlfriend," Barney said.

"I'm not his girlfriend," I said.

"Even better," Barney leered. "You're too sexy for him

and he's too young for you. You need a man who can show you what your body can do?"

He draped an arm around my shoulder and pulled me in close.

"We need to get to the south stage," Osbert said, pulling me away from Barney. "We'll see you later."

Barney rubbed my ass and promised to find me later.

"Please don't let him near me again," I whispered to Osbert.

"Absolutely not," Osbert promised.

Osbert hadn't been lying. There was a band we wanted to see on the south stage, but we needed to push our way through the throngs of people. It felt like there were even more people that day than the day before. "Is it just me or are there more people here?" I asked.

Osbert looked around. "Yeah, it definitely feels more crowded."

We got to the stage and over the next few hours, the place grew even more packed with people. "I think we should head back to our tent," Osbert said. He was surveying the crowd with a wary eye.

Alcohol was forbidden, yet we could see people carrying cases of beer.

"Where did they get the beer?" I asked.

"I don't know," Osbert said. "They're getting drunk, though."

There was a rowdy group of men blocking the paths of women, demanding "Show us your tits."

Barney seemed downright harmless compared to those Neanderthals.

"Let's go. I want to find my brother," I said. I'd barely kept tabs on C.B. all weekend because I felt like we were in a fairly safe environment. But now, the mood and energy of the crowd had shifted. The rain continued to come down and the whole place was a mud pit.

We were pressed together moving in a slow conga line back toward the north stage and our tent when Osbert said, "Okay, seriously, there are twice as many people here now than this morning. Where the fuck did everyone come from?"

The guy in front of me looked over his shoulder and said, "The gates are down and security has quit. It's a fucking free-for-all, man."

"What?" I asked.

"Yeah, radio DJs are telling people they can get in for free, so people are just coming up here from all over. They pushed the fences down and I heard the food has run out."

"It's going to turn into *Lord of the Flies*," I said.

"I didn't see that movie," the guy said.

I knew it was only a two-hour drive from the New York City metro area to Saugerties, so I wasn't surprised by the influx of people. But I was concerned.

"I want to find my brother right now," I said.

"I know," Osbert said, peering over my head. "We're almost there. I can see Barney and Bev. Ew. I think they're fucking in the mud."

"Super," I said.

When we got to the tent, my brother and Roland weren't there. I hadn't specifically told C.B. to stay with the tent, but I just assumed he would. We didn't have cellphones, so I didn't know how to find him.

"He'll come back soon," Osbert assured me. "I told him and Roland to check in with us every couple of hours."

"That was smart," I said.

There was a loud crash and I watched with horror as the wet and soggy ground beneath the port-a-potties gave way, causing them to tumble down the muddy hill, dumping their contents everywhere.

"Do you think anyone was in there?" I asked.

"No," Osbert said. "They overflowed yesterday."

As the evening wore on, the concert became more and more crowded. According to later news reports, only 164,000 tickets had been sold but it was estimated the crowd swelled to over 550,000 people. I became increasingly worried.

When my brother and Roland finally emerged out of the darkness, covered head to toe in mud, I grabbed them both and hugged them. "Where were you?" I demanded.

"The mosh pit," C.B. said. "It's amazing. I think I got a black eye."

"No more mosh pit," I ordered. "This place is turning into a fucking zoo. No one leaves the tent from now on."

C.B. and Roland didn't argue with me.

Now that I had the teenagers back, I turned my attention to the other issue bugging me: "How are we going to get out of here?" I asked.

"What do you mean?" Osbert said.

"Well, the first night there were only a few thousand of us and we still had to wait in line for thirty minutes to catch a bus. And then the bus ride was twenty minutes. Now there are so many more people here. Even if they double the number of buses, what's going to happen tomorrow morning when we all try to catch those buses?"

Osbert frowned. "Yeah, I hadn't really thought about that."

I was pleasantly surprised that for once I was the one thinking ahead. "How far away do you think the field is where we parked? Could we walk?" I asked.

Osbert shook his head. "It was a twenty-minute ride. So maybe ten or fifteen miles?"

"Fuck, that's far," I said.

"Yeah," he agreed.

By that time, Barney and Bev were back from their love-making session in the mud (and shit) and they joined our group. "Why so serious?" Barney asked, throwing an arm around my shoulders.

I shrugged him off. "We're trying to figure out how to get out of here tomorrow. It's going to be a logistical nightmare with all these extra people."

"We're going to walk it," Bev said.

"I think it's too far to walk," I said.

Bev shook her head. "No, it won't be bad. It's only two miles to the VIP lot."

"Hang on," I said. "You're VIPs too?"

Barney nodded. "Of course. I represent two of the bands here."

"You're a lawyer?" C.B. exclaimed.

Bev looked offended. "Only one of the best," she said. "He went to Harvard for fuck's sake."

I didn't care about Barney's pedigree, I wanted to know more about this VIP parking lot. In all the information Dad had given me, nowhere did it say there was a special parking lot for us. "Where's the VIP lot?" I asked.

"It's in town," Barney said.

"We don't have the address or anything," Bev said.

"But you can walk to it," I said.

"Yeah, we walked here from it," Barney said.

Osbert and I exchanged a look. "If you could move the Jeep," he said.

"Then we could walk to the car when the concert ends," I said.

We decided that Osbert and I would get up early in the morning and catch the first bus to the main parking area and then we'd move the car to the VIP lot. "We'll come back and help you guys pack," I told C.B. "But stay at the tent. Don't leave the tent. Do you understand?"

THE NEXT MORNING Osbert and I were in the bus line right after sunrise. We were shocked to see so many people had obviously done the same complicated math I had done, realizing they needed to get the fuck out as soon as possible.

The buses weren't running on any kind of schedule. One would pull up and a fuck ton of people would pile on with all their shit. When they couldn't fit, they were dumping backpacks and tents and coolers so they could press on.

As the morning went on, the buses started running even more sporadically. The bands had started playing and the rumor was that many of the bus drivers had abandoned their posts to enjoy the concert.

Osbert and I were about to give up when I spotted a bus idling a few hundred feet away. I nudged him, motioning for him to follow me. We didn't have anything to carry, so we could move fast. Well, as fast as someone can move when they're traversing through twelve inches of mud. We got to the bus and I banged on the doors until the driver opened them. "I'm off-duty," he said.

I flashed the VIP badge around my neck and said, "Fuck that, I'm a VIP and I need to get to my car." Now, I'm not usually one to be a total asshole, but desperate times call for desperate measures. We hadn't seen another bus in over an hour and I needed to commandeer this one. I hauled my ass up the stairs and put on my bitchiest face. "Don't make me call my father," I said.

The driver looked me up and down. I was a hot fucking mess. I knew I didn't look like anything much, but I figured it was all in the attitude and I had attitude to spare. "Who's your dad?" the driver asked.

Without thinking, I blurted out, "Tommy Mottola." I really didn't know who Tommy Mottola was except I'd heard Dad talking about him. I knew the tickets came from a friend of a friend of a friend of Tommy Mottola. Maybe?

"Never heard of him," the driver said.

"He's married to Mariah Carey," Osbert said.

"You're telling me your mom is Mariah Carey?"

I cringed. "She's my step-mom," I said.

The driver rolled his eyes. "Whatever." He glanced as his watch. "You're in luck. My break's over. Let's get your where you need to go, Mariah's step-kid."

Osbert and I took the nearest seats and let out a huge sigh of relief.

The bus lurched and we were off. We drove right past the line of people we'd just been waiting with, but the driver didn't slow down.

"Are you going to stop for them?" Osbert asked.

"Nah, you fucking people stink. It's gross. The fewer, the better," the driver said.

As the crowd realized the bus wasn't stopping for them, they became enraged and quickly turned into a mob. They swarmed the bus, hitting the sides and rattling the doors, demanding to be let inside. People threw empty water bottles and shoes at us. Osbert and I kept our heads down. The driver barely hit the brakes and the sea of people parted.

Within twenty minutes we were looking for our Jeep in

a field of cars. It wasn't like Disneyland where you have some sort of identifier to let you know where you left your car. We weren't in Red Mickey Mouse, Row 118. We were in a goddamn muddy field of thousands of cars. Some were in neat rows, others looked abandoned. Some were completely blocked in. I hadn't thought about that possibility at all!

"Okay," Osbert said. "We'll divide and conquer. You go that way. I'll go this way. Yell when you find the car."

I don't remember how long we were out there, but it felt like hours. I was exhausted from slogging through the mud and scared I'd never get home. Finally, I heard Osbert yell, "I found it!"

"Oh thank god!" I yelled. I ran toward him, but I got stuck in an especially gooey mound of mud. Instead of sinking up to my knees like normal, I found myself stuck up to my thighs! It was like quicksand.

"Jen!" Osbert yelled. "Where are you?"

"I'm here!" I screamed. "I'm stuck in the mud!"

Osbert found me dragging myself out of the quagmire. I'd gotten one leg out but my other leg wasn't budging. "Here," he said. "Let me help." He pushed and pulled me until finally the mud released me with a loud smack. I landed on the ground with my leg in the air. My sock and my shoe were gone. Someday archaeologists will find them and speculate on how they got there.

"Let's get the fuck out of here," I said, pulling myself off the ground. "Where's the car?"

I followed Osbert to the other side of the field where I saw the most glorious sight. There was my beautiful, lovely, familiar Jeep with a clear path out of the parking lot. I practically kissed the hood.

"Can you drive?" Osbert asked.

I was missing my right sock and shoe, but other than that, I was good. I needed him to navigate. Bev had given us some rudimentary directions and Osbert had a better sense of direction than I did. "I'm good," I said.

We'd made it a few miles when we hit the first State Police roadblock. The officer waved us over to the side and motioned for me to roll down my window.

"You local?" he asked.

I thought about lying, but we were driving a car with Kansas plates and we were covered in mud. "No, sir," I said.

"This road is for locals only."

"Is this the way to the VIP parking lot?" I asked.

"You're a VIP?" he asked.

I flashed the badge around my neck. "Yes, sir."

"Okay," he said. "Next time, lead with that, kid." He waved us through.

For the next two roadblocks, I just flashed my badge and no one stopped us. But then we got to the fourth roadblock in the middle of town. I flashed my badge, but the officer still signaled for me to pull over.

He walked up to my window, looking like something out of central casting, right down to the Ray Bans and a toothpick in the corner of his mouth. "You need to turn this vehicle around," he said.

"No, sir," I said. "We're going to the VIP parking lot."

"I don't know anything about that," he said.

Osbert pointed excitedly. "There it is! I can see it!"

Sure enough, I could see a handwritten sandwich board sign a few blocks away pointing out the entrance to the VIP lot.

"We've VIPs," I said. "We need to park there."

The cop pulled the toothpick out of his mouth and

threw it on the ground. "You need a parking pass to park there. That thing around your neck isn't a parking pass."

"No, it's okay," I said. "I was told this was fine."

"Who told you?" he asked.

"T-t-t-ommy Mottola," I stuttered.

I could sense Osbert tensing up. I knew he was mad at me for pulling the Tommy Mottola card again, but it had worked last time, maybe it would work again?

"Tommy Mottola. Mariah Carey's husband? *He* told you that you could park there?"

"Um...his secretary did," I squeaked.

"How do you know Tommy Mottola?" the cop asked.

This guy seemed a bit brighter than the bus driver. I didn't think I could get away with calling Tommy Mottola my dad again, so this time I said, "He's my godfather."

"You've got Kansas plates on this car," the cop said. "How does a girl from Kansas end up with Tommy Mottola for a godfather?"

I knew my opportunity was slipping away and I was going to have to do something drastic if we were going to get to that parking lot. I called up the memory and attitude of the amazing Brigitte combined with every obnoxious, bitchy, entitled, spoiled girl I could think of and channeled it into one sentence. "My dad, Barney, has been Mariah's lawyer for years," I said. I scrutinized the badge on the officer's shirt and continued. "In fact, my dad is backstage right now with Bob Dylan. He asked me to move his car for him and that's what I'm *trying* to do. I'm not sure what the problem is here, but I'm positive my dad would *love* to have a conversation about this with your supervisor, Officer Cline."

The police officer and I stared at one another and I could tell he didn't believe a word I said. I could also tell he was completely out of fucks to give. He'd probably been sitting there all weekend dealing with assholes like me and it was the afternoon of the final day. The end was finally in sight. He scoffed but waved us through.

TWO HOURS later we were back at the concert pulling C.B. and Roland out of the mosh pit. "I told you to stay at the fucking tent," I growled.

"It was Green Day, Jen!" C.B. argued, as if that made a difference to me.

When the concert was over we trudged through the mud with Barney and Bev to the VIP lot. We said goodbye and never saw them again. The ride home was a blur. I only clearly remember stopping at a friend's house in Pennsylvania for a shower and nap. (I still owe her a pair of Keds to replace the ones she gave me.) When Osbert and I returned the tent, we waited nervously for the manager to freak out over the condition of his property. It was covered in mud (and shit) and ripped in several places. The window was shredded and the door was tattered. We were missing several stakes and a pole had snapped.

I hung my head in shame and did the calculations, figuring my credit card would be charged several hundred dollars for the damage. But I hadn't needed to worry, because the manager exclaimed, "This is so fucking cool! Look at this thing! Our tent was at Woodstock! I'm displaying this in the front window!"

And, finally, I feel like I owe Tommy Mottola and Mariah Carey apologies for name-dropping them all weekend. But without their help we'd probably still be waiting for a bus at Winston Farm.

FIVE

A VERY BIG PRESENT FOR A VERY A BIG REASON

KIEV, UKRAINE

1995

The summer after my senior year in college I was studying abroad in Kiev, Ukraine. The Berlin Wall had fallen only a few years before and many Eastern Bloc countries like Ukraine still had very few comforts of home. (It was the mid- 1990s, so McDonald's hadn't even arrived yet!) Before I left the States, I'd been warned that many of the day-to-day items we could just pick up at the drug store would not be available in my new city of Kiev. I was advised to pack all the essentials I would need for the entire time I'd be there. So, I loaded up an additional suitcase with all the indispensable items: toilet paper, soap, toothpaste, and, most importantly, tampons.

I quickly figured out my American roommate, Kasey, had ignored that part of the packing list and arrived in Ukraine ill-prepared. Unsurprisingly, on our first day in Kiev, Kasey received her monthly bill and freaked out.

That morning she emerged from our bathroom in a panic. "Do you have any tampons?" she asked.

I'll be completely honest: I was a reluctant to share. Partly because I'm an asshole and partly because I knew I'd only packed enough for me. I was pissed at her for being so irresponsible. I had done the right thing and packed much-needed essentials. Kasey didn't bring tampons, but she did bring a fuck ton of condoms and breath mints. When I'd commented on her stash the night before she said, "Eastern European men love American women. We're going to get so many men." I had not read that in my tourist guide, but I figured I'd take her word for it.

"I need to check how many I have," I said, hesitantly. I knew my period wasn't due for another couple of weeks, so I'd have time to (hopefully) find a drugstore and replenish my stash.

"You can help yourself to my breath mints," Kasey offered, helpfully. I noticed her offer didn't extend to her condom stash.

I rifled in my suitcase for a bit. "I only have a couple," I lied. "Did you ask Olga?"

Olga was our primary contact with the university. We'd been told that whatever we needed, Olga could get.

"Yeah, I talked to her last night once I realized the date. She gave me these." Kasey tossed a plastic grocery bag at me.

I looked inside and saw it was full of rags.

"What the hell?" I asked.

"Now I know where the phrase 'on the rag' comes from," Kasey said, shuddering.

"Wait," I said, looking up from the bag. "You mean, these are for..."

"Yeah," Kasey spat. "I literally have rags stuffed in my pants right now, Jen! Now do you understand why I'm so desperate?"

"Oh shit," I said.

"Yeah! Let me have two or three tampons, please. I'm

miserable. Olga said she'd take shopping today. I'll buy you a whole box."

My inner asshole was screaming, *"No, Jen! You know better. You were warned! She won't be able to find tampons anywhere. Even Olga doesn't have tampons! Pretty soon you'll be the one bleeding on rags, you dumb bitch, because you gave Kasey all your tampons!"*

But I was softer and gentler back then. I felt bad for Kasey and cringed at the thought of her walking around with one of Olga's homemade pads stuffed in her drawers. I was positive the dire warnings I'd received were just fear-mongering. Kiev was a huge, bustling city. Surely, there were tampons out there somewhere!

"Okay," I said. Warily I handed over two of my precious tampons. "Olga's taking you out today, right?"

Kasey grabbed the tampons greedily and nodded. "Absolutely. She said it might take us a few trips, though. They're a little scarce right now."

"What?" I said. "You made it sound like Olga knew where to go."

"I'm sure she has an idea. Don't worry. I will buy you two boxes to pay you back!"

That evening Kasey returned to our dorm room empty-handed. Well, not completely empty-handed. She'd found more condoms. "They're lambskin!" she exclaimed. I must have looked disappointed because she added, "I got you some too!"

"I thought Olga knew where to go," I said.

Kasey shrugged. "She only took me to one store and then told me to stop being so spoiled. I guess this is the true Ukrainian experience, right?" Kasey was rooting around in my suitcase.

"What are you doing?" I asked.

"Well, I did bring you like six condoms. That's worth another two tampons, right?"

I didn't need condoms. I needed tampons!

No matter where I hid my box of tampons the next week, Kasey managed to find it. "Hey, Jen, I took a couple tampons. But I left you some breath mints. Don't worry, we're totally going to settle up. I'll be buying you tampons for a year!"

I didn't know if Kasey had an unusually heavy flow or if she was making tampon crafts, but by the end of the week, my resources were decimated.

"I'm almost out," I cried, shaking the nearly empty box at Kasey. "And I start next week!"

"I told you," Kasey reassured me. "I'm going to make it right."

EVERY DAY KASEY and I would go into the city and every day we looked for a place to purchase tampons. We had a hard time deciphering the Cyrillic alphabet, but we quickly learned that *"apteka"* meant pharmacy. To us, a pharmacy was the most logical place to sell tampons.

"Look, there's an *apteka*," I said one morning as we were walking to class. By then I was edging closer to my own visit with Aunt Flow, but at least I had an overabundance of breath mints and condoms. "Let's stop in and see what they have."

We found a small store with a limited supply of pills, creams, and ointments, but no tampons.

The pharmacist could speak a little English and asked if he could help us. I was embarrassed to tell him what I needed and I could see from his half-empty shelves he wasn't hiding anything in the storeroom.

"She needs tampons," Kasey said, confidently. I wanted to sink into the floor and die.

The pharmacist looked at me quizzically. He didn't understand.

Kasey tried again. "Sanitary napkins?"

Sanitary napkins? I thought. *I hadn't worn a pad since middle school, but they would have to do.*

The pharmacist led us to the bandage aisle. "Napkins?" he said, helpfully.

Not even close, but if things got desperate, it was good to know there were some pretty good-sized gauze pads for wounds. Maybe they'd be absorbent enough? *"Spasibo,"* I muttered.

"Yeah, thanks," Kasey said. When we stepped outside the doors Kasey exclaimed, "Well, at least I still have all those unused rags from Olga. You're welcome to them, of course."

Oh fuck you, Kasey, I thought. *And fuck you, Jen, for being too damn nice to Kasey.*

I was officially up shit creek.

In the meantime, I'd met a cute boy, Alexei, and I was busy flirting awkwardly with him rather than focusing on the pressing need that was coming in seven short days. Every time he took me out he asked if I'd like to see anything special. I didn't know what to ask for, exactly. I knew the *apteka* wasn't the right place to find tampons, but I didn't know where else to look. So I asked him to show me all the "special" types of stores that sold interesting and unique items.

He took me to an antiques store. I realized I needed to change my approach.

"No," I said. "Maybe a grocery store?"

"You want food?" Alexei asked. "I will take you to dinner."

"No, I just want to browse the aisles," I said.

Alexei frowned. "There is not much to see there unless you want food," he said.

"Show me," I begged.

He wasn't lying. The grocery store only had a few loaves of bread, some root vegetables, tons of canned products, and a small butcher area. Not even close to what I needed.

I asked for a "woman's store."

"What does this mean? Woman's store?" he asked, pulling out his handy Russian to English dictionary he carried everywhere. Alexei's English was perfect. It was my refusal to come clean with what I needed that was causing our language barrier.

I was way too embarrassed. Alexei was cute and funny and we had fun together. I didn't want to make it weird by talking about my bodily functions and the fact that I needed a tube of cotton to shove up my hooha.

Of course Alexei couldn't understand what the fuck I was talking about. As we got closer to the big red circle on my calendar, I'd run into any random store I saw that I had not been in already.

Finally, it was almost p-day and panic was setting in. Alexei could obviously feel my anxiety. He sat me down and said, "Jen, please let me help you. Simply tell me what you are looking for. I can help you find it." Again I was too self-conscious to tell him, so I refused.

"Jen, it is upsetting you and I want to help you. Maybe it is a special souvenir of Kiev you would like?"

I practically laughed. A souvenir? No, Alexei, not even close.

The morning before Mother Nature's Gift was scheduled to make her appearance I woke up to find the bag of rags on my desk. Obviously, Kasey had been paying attention to the calendar too. I almost cried thinking about ramming a scrap of Olga's husbands old t-shirts in my crotch, so I finally broke down at lunch and told Alexei what I needed.

It only took his Russian to English dictionary, a little bit of charades, and finally a hand drawn picture of various Kotex, O.B., and Tampax boxes to help him understand.

"Do you know where I can find these?" I asked hopefully, showing him my crude artwork.

Alexei studied my drawing closely and finally nodded. "Yes," he replied. "But it will be very expensive. You can only get them on the black market."

I nearly cried with relief. "I don't care, Alexei! I need them. I'll pay. I have U.S. dollars. How much will it cost?"

Alexei winced. "I do not know. Maybe twenty?" he said.

We were eating a $3 pizza, so $20 was a shit load of money in Kiev. Twenty dollars felt like a bargain in exchange for my dignity. "Fine. Whatever. Let's go right now and get them," I said, like the black market was a 24-hour Walmart where I could grab some tampons along with a bag of chips and some batteries.

Alexei laughed. "There's nowhere to go. It is not a place, Jen. I will need to ask my friends. It will take me some time."

"But I need them by tomorrow."

"I will do my best," Alexei promised.

We arranged for him to go and see what he could find and then meet later that night at a dorm party.

I got to the party before him and was hanging with my

new cool European friends when Alexei walked in with a plastic shopping bag. "Jen," he said. "I have a gift for you."

Relief swept over me. "Great, Alexei. Thanks so much. I owe ya," I said. I tried to swipe the bag from him before everyone could see what he had brought me.

"No, Jen," he said pulling the bag out of my reach. "In this country, gifts are very special. You must be presented just right or else the gift is spoiled." He straightened his spine and fixed his face into a solemn, stoic expression.

It felt like everyone in the room stopped what they were doing to watch Alexei's formal presentation. I'm sure my memory is faulty, but I could swear even the music stopped playing so people could hear better.

What the fuck is happening? I thought.

"I don't want a gift, Alexei. I will pay you for them," I hissed. I was partially embarrassed that Alexei was trying to make a box of tampons into a gift, but I was even more concerned that he'd spent a king's ransom to get them. I had fifty bucks (and a condom) shoved in my back pocket. Of course, twenty bucks was a lot for me to spend on a box of tampons but for Alexei, twenty dollars could be a whole month's salary.

"No," Alexei said. "I insist. Our time together is almost over. You'll be returning to the United States soon and I have not bought you anything to remember me by. I did not know what to get you. You are someone who has everything. But this is something you need more than anything and so I want to give you this as a gift." He thrust the shopping bag toward me with such pageantry I felt like it was an engagement ring. "For you, Jen. To remember me and to remember Kiev."

Everyone pushed in close and gathered around to see what amazing gift my new cute boyfriend was giving me to remember him by. Their faces were lit up with excitement and questions.

What could it be?

Jewelry?

A book of romantic poetry?

A love letter?

A framed photograph of the two of you?

I was dying inside.

Remember you? Are you kidding me? They're tampons, dude. I'm not going to save one to remember you by.

Alexei made a huge production of pulling out a giant box of Tampax tampons and held it up like the fucking monkey holding up Simba in *The Lion King*. A girl in the back gasped and another one said, "Ooooh."

Alexei took a deep breath and announced, "Jen Mann, I present to you this gift of Tampax."

I looked around the room and caught a glimpse of Kasey giggling in a corner. *Fucking Kasey,* I thought. *This is all your fault. I'm going to make you pay Alexei fifty bucks!*

Alexei continued, "It is my pleasure to give you this gift. I got you the big box. I did not know how many you would need. But you are a big girl, Jen, and I thought you might have a big menses."

I don't remember much of the night after that. I do know Kasey never paid Alexei, she swore he wouldn't take her money, which was probably true. I also know Alexei was absolutely right. His gift was one of the most memorable gifts I've ever received in my entire life. I've never forgotten him and every time I pull out a box of Tampax, I think of him and offer him a little word of thanks.

Spasibo, Alexei.

SIX

SOMEONE WILL BREAK A HIP IF THEY'RE NOT CAREFUL!

TALLINN, ESTONIA

2002

While I planned the bulk of the wedding and our move from New York City to Kansas City, the Hubs worked hard on the honeymoon.

Throughout my life, when I've thought of the word "honeymoon," I think of warm destinations—pristine beaches, cabanas, cold drinks. Specifically, those huts in Bali you see on the cover of *Conde Nast Traveler* that sit on stilts out in the ocean. To me, *that's* always been what a honeymoon should be.

My skin is super fair, though, and allergic to sunscreen. So I'm like a vampire at the beach. When I'm outside, I need to cower in any sort of shade I can find. So I imagined myself in my warm-destination honeymoon sitting in the shadiest part of my raised bungalow's deck, hidden under an enormous hat, cold drink in one hand and a great book in the other.

You're probably wondering where the Hubs fits into this fantasy. I know he always wonders. Well, he enjoys snorkeling and I do not (can you imagine my pasty white backside at the end of a day of snorkeling? No thank you!), so he would be floating around under our little retreat enjoying the fish and coming up every now and again to tell me what I'm missing.

Even though The Hubs loves snorkeling, he hated my Bali idea. He reminded me we were both unemployed at that point. We couldn't afford traveling to Bali then spending $600 a night to sleep out in the ocean where we'd toss and turn all night worrying about one rogue wave that might wipe us off the map. So that fantasy honeymoon idea got nixed pretty quickly. *No worries,* I thought. There are plenty of other beaches in the world.

And then I realized I was marrying a man I barely knew. Before we even got engaged, we'd had in-depth discussions about the pros and cons of spanking our future children (we are anti-spanking), what we'd do in the event of one of us getting hit by a bus and becoming paralyzed (the paralyzed person would communicate through rapid blinking), the boundaries we would set with my mom and dad once we moved within five miles of their house (always call before you drop by), but we'd never discussed beach vacations.

Let me be clear about what I mean when I say "beaches." I actually despise sand. I like walking on it just fine (if it's not too hot) and I'll even enjoy a quick frolic in the surf (if it's not too cold, too fishy, too seaweed-y, or too rough). But I abhor laying out at the beach where the slightest breeze blows grains of sand into my eyes and my nether regions. And I really don't care for swimming much in the ocean because there are way too many fish and shadows that look like sharks. But I do love a beautiful hotel with an ocean view and a bevy of gorgeous pools (with giant umbrellas to hide under). My place is by the pool with my books and magazines. Sand-free and close to a bathroom and the bar.

The Hubs thinks this sounds like torture. He prefers to snorkel, fish, cliff dive, and take a helicopter ride—all in the same damn day. When he's sitting by the pool all he can do is calculate in his head how much this relaxing time is costing him per minute. "We can relax at home for free!" is always his argument.

Picking a honeymoon destination was the first compromise of many we'd have to make in our marriage. I didn't want to go anywhere resort-y if I wasn't going to be able to relax and enjoy it, and somehow, bicycling down the side of a dormant volcano did not sound relaxing to me! The Hubs thought Europe sounded good, but he was only willing to go to a country I'd never been to. "I want us to experience a place for the first time together," he said. I'm a bit of a traveler, so that was a tough one.

We pulled out a map of Europe and studied it closely. "What about England?" he asked.

"I went there in high school," I replied. I pulled out a Sharpie so I could cross out England.

"Oh yeah. And we did France together last year."

"Yes," I said, marking an X through France.

"Just go ahead and mark everywhere you've been and then we'll see what we have left," the Hubs said.

I eliminated Italy, Germany, and Austria. Spain and Portugal got the ax next. And then I finished up by giving Switzerland, Belgium, Denmark, Poland, Czech, Bulgaria, and Ukraine the old heave ho.

"I'm pretty sure I'm no longer banned from Hungary," I said. "But I'd rather not risk it on our honeymoon."

"What's left?" the Hubs asked, peering at the map.

"All kinds of places," I said. "What about Scotland? I've always wanted to go to Scotland."

The Hubs wrinkled his nose. "I don't know. It feels so ordinary. I'd like to go somewhere unusual."

"Unusual? What do you mean?"

He shrugged. "I don't know. Just some place different. Some place no one would expect. Besides Scotland, where is another place you've wanted to go?"

We looked at the map again and then I pointed to a small country in northeastern Europe. "Estonia," I said.

"Never heard of it," the Hubs said.

I bet some of you are saying you've never heard of it either. Boy, there are some geography teachers out there crying right now.

I'm going to sound like a paid spokesperson for the tourism bureau of Estonia, but I don't really care. Tallinn, Estonia has been on my list of must-see cities for my whole life. I have this weird fascination with Tallinn's medieval city. Tallinn is one of the oldest capitals in Europe and although it was part of the Soviet Bloc for years, it was left virtually untouched. It overlooks the Gulf of Finland and has a fully preserved medieval town full of restaurants, shops, and art galleries. It looks like something out of a fairy tale. I felt like it was the perfect choice for anyone's honeymoon: beautiful and romantic. But I'll warn you, it's cold as hell in October—so bring a hat!

Once I was done giving the Hubs my Tallinn pitch, he said, "Well, that certainly sounds unusual. Let's do it!"

A FEW MONTHS later we arrived in Tallinn and it was just as pretty as I'd imagined. We'd picked a small, boutique hotel near the center of town and when we arrived, the manager was waiting to greet us.

"Welcome!" he said. "Happy marriage!"

"I'll check us in," the Hubs said, leaving me with the luggage.

There was some quiet discussion back and forth and finally a bellman grabbed our bags. I was exhausted from traveling and dreaming of a hot shower and nap before dinner out in the city. We hopped on the elevator and were whisked to the top floor. The door dinged and the bellman stepped off, holding the doors for us.

"Top floor?" I said. "Oooh. Did you get a suite or something?"

The Hubs just smiled.

We followed the bellman to the end of a long, winding hallway where we were greeted by three of the most Eastern European babushkas I've ever seen. They sat on little wooden stools lined up right outside our room door chattering away in Estonian. I can't be sure, but it looked (and smelled) like they were swilling vodka out of paper cups.

The bellman motioned to the women. "It is cleaning help," he explained.

"I see," I said.

As I walked by, one of the women winked at me and then turned and spoke in Estonian to the bellman.

He nodded and said, "All is prepared for you." He opened our door and dropped our bags right inside the door. I turned to thank and tip him, but he'd disappeared.

"Weird," I said, stuffing the dollar bills back in my pocket.

"What do you think?" the Hubs asked, grinning foolishly.

I turned around and looked at the small room. The two of us and our suitcases barely fit around the main focal point: a king size bed completely done up in ruffled, baby blue silk sheets. Six pillows (all covered in baby blue silk) were perfectly plumped and propped against the wooden headboard. Red rose petals formed a giant heart in the middle of the bed with the leftovers strewn around it like confetti. It looked like the set of a bad Russian porn film.

"What the hell is that?" I scoffed.

"I arranged for it," said the Hubs, his face falling. "I thought you might like it. It's romantic."

"Is it?" I asked, immediately feeling bad. He'd tried so hard and I could see this was not the reaction he was looking for. "Oh, I'm sorry. I didn't realize you were serious." In my defense, the Hubs is not known for romantic overtures. He's never been the type of guy to read me poetry or write me a love song. He didn't even make me a mixed tape when we were dating! Standing next to the rose covered bed, I didn't know how to behave. Sarcasm was my love language, not silk sheets!

"It's our honeymoon," the Hubs said. "The manager and I thought this would be fun."

I frowned. "It looks...slippery."

The Hubs smiled. "Yeah it does. Come on, Jen." He pulled me close. "Let's find out."

I let him embrace me and tried to let myself go and make myself appreciate his rarely seen romantic side.

Tee hee hee.

I pulled away. "What was that?"

"What was what?" he asked, clearly ready to destroy those silk sheets. He kissed me and I tried to get back in the moment.

Tee hee hee.

I stopped kissing him. "That! Can't you hear that?"

"Hear what?"

I put a finger to my lips and said, "Shh, listen. Someone is laughing at us!"

"No one is laughing at us."

Tee hee hee.

This time I was paying close attention and I could tell it came from outside our door. "Oh my God! It's the babushkas in the hallway," I whispered. "They're laughing at us. They're the ones who set this up in here and now they're waiting for the show. They can hear us!"

"They can't hear us," the Hubs said, reaching for me again.

"Shh," I said, swatting away his hands.

Tee hee hee.

That time the Hubs heard them too. "Oh shit, they *can* hear us!"

"See?" I hissed. "What the hell?" I was equal parts annoyed and embarrassed. I had a vision of the three of them making the rose petal heart on our bed and taking bets on whether or not I'd get knocked up that night. Any sort of excitement and desire I'd felt moments before evaporated.

But the Hubs didn't give a fuck about the old ladies outside the door. He was ready to get the honeymoon started, with or without an audience. "Who cares?" he said, nuzzling my neck. "Let them listen. Maybe they'll learn something."

"Oh my god, stop!" I shoved him. "We can *not* do this with them outside the door. That is so fucking creepy!"

Now the Hubs was irritated. "Oh who cares, Jen? They can't even speak English. They won't know what's going on."

"You don't think they understand, 'Oh yeah, baby'? Of

course they understand! Sex is a universal language and the hell I can get busy with those three snickering and taking vodka shots right outside my door. No way!" I said.

"So, what do you want to do, then?" the Hubs asked.

"I'm exhausted. Let's take a nap. They should be gone by the time we wake up," I said. "I promise I'll be a good wife after a nap."

The Hubs looked distraught. "You want to take a nap on our honeymoon?" he asked.

"Naps are actually more romantic than sex," I argued. "You can have sex with anyone, but you have to be very close to want to nap together."

The Hubs looked skeptical. "If you say so."

We carefully scooped the rose petals into the trash can and got into bed. I was right about those damn slippery sheets! I'd never experienced anything like it. One quick roll over and you could be out on the floor before you even knew what hit you. I could barely stay in the bed just napping! Someone was going to break a hip having sex in those suckers.

As soon as we got up from our nap I called house-keeping and asked them for some nice cotton sheets. "Are you sure you want other sheets?" the woman on the line asked with a thick Eastern European accent. "Is not as good for the sex."

I'd just have to take her word for it.

SEVEN

IN SICKNESS AND IN HEALTH

STOCKHOLM, SWEDEN

2002

We'd been married about two whole weeks when my wedding vows were tested. We'd spent most of our honeymoon in Tallinn but tacked on a couple of days in Stockholm, Sweden. The Hubs had originally booked us a room in one of the swankiest hotels in Stockholm. He was quite proud of himself and I think I burst his bubble when I caught a glimpse of the room rates and flipped out. He'd spent a huge portion of our budget on a beautiful room with a view of the Söderström and I was pissed off.

"Why would you do that?" I demanded.

He was shocked. "I thought you'd like it," he insisted. "It's romantic."

"It's not romantic, it's a waste," I argued. "I can't believe how much you spent on this room. And it's not even that nice!"

"What do you mean?"

"Look around! It's really kind of shabby when you look closely. Yes, the view is gorgeous and the room is spacious, but the furniture is drab and the carpets worn and the bed lumpy. For what this cost we could have gone on more excursions or had nicer meals. I can't believe you did this."

Looking back now, it's kind of amazing he didn't leave me right then and there. What a bitch, right? I mean, this was my honeymoon and it was the second time I was acting like Bridezilla because my husband tried to do something nice for me. I was being a total twat about it.

But then again, I wasn't. Because I promise you: He didn't do that for me. This is the same man who used a coupon on our first date. The man who will go five miles out of his way to save a nickel per gallon on gas. He's also a man who gets all caught up in the shit he reads in those fancy magazines. I was positive he'd read about this hotel in some high-end travel magazine and was like, "Ohh, I must stay there!" Because that's how he thinks. He's the cheapest decadent man out there. He's a label whore who shops at the outlet mall and this was no different. He saw this hotel on the travel channel or some dumb shit and wanted something to brag about. That's why he booked it. Not to impress me. Not at all.

He took a closer look around the room and he could see I was right. He tugged on a loose thread on the curtains and dug his toe into the moth-eaten rug. "You're right," he said. "Who do these people think they are charging me so much for this shit hole?"

"Hang on," I said, trying to calm him down. "Shit hole is a strong word." I was feeling bad and I wanted to diffuse the situation a bit.

"You don't even know, Jen," he said. "This is considered a suite. I paid even more than you think."

I was horrified. "You did?"

"Yeah! I think I was duped. This looks nothing like the

website. This looks nothing like the brochure. I want my money back!"

Yeah, fuck being nice. I wanted my money back now, too—or at least some kind of discount maybe.

We trekked down the front desk and the Hubs demanded to speak to whomever was in charge.

"You can speak to me, sir," the man behind the desk said.

"Are you in charge?"

"How can I help you, sir?"

And then the Hubs launched into a tirade about how he'd been hoodwinked and was furious. (He wasn't furious, but he's a New Yorker and he can pull attitude on demand.) "Our room looks nothing like the pictures on the internet," he said.

"The pictures on the internet show the renovated portion of the hotel."

"Well, we wanted a renovated room, then," he said.

"Sir, you indicated you preferred a higher floor with a view of the river. The renovations are starting on the lower floors."

"Well, someone should have told me that when I booked the room. You should have asked me if I wanted a renovated room."

The man shrugged as if to say, "Buyer beware."

When the Hubs could see that the disagreement wasn't going his way, and he wasn't getting what he felt he was due, he implied our honeymoon was ruined.

Actually, he didn't imply it, he said it. "You have ruined our honeymoon. Look at my wife. She's devastated."

By now the Hubs had pitched such a fit that we had three people attending to us and everyone turned to look at me and I tried to look devastated, but it was really hard, because really I was just fucking pissed that we'd spent so much money and we weren't going to get it back.

"I'm sorry, madame," the man said.

"Sorry's not enough. What are you going to do to make it up to her?"

The man shrugged again. "There is nothing we can do. You've already stayed one night. We cannot refund when you've already taken advantage of the hotel and all of its fine amenities."

I scoffed at that one. Fine amenities. That was a joke. There was nothing except matches and shampoo to take advantage of and I'd already stolen all the shampoo I could carry.

"What if we check out now?" the Hubs asked.

I squeaked a bit. We were in a foreign city without a clue where to go.

"If you checked out now, sir, we would only charge you for last night and not charge you for the remainder of your stay."

"Fine! Let's do that," the Hubs said. "We'll go back to pack and be out in twenty minutes."

He turned on his heel and stalked off toward the elevator while I chased after him.

"What are you doing?" I whispered.

"Making a scene," he whispered. "Don't worry, they'll cave. It's four o'clock. No one is going to rent our room tonight. Maybe not even tomorrow. That guy doesn't want to lose our business. They'll give us a discount, you'll see. I bet we'll have a message by the time we get to our room."

Only we didn't have a message when we got to our room. We opened the door and the little message light on the phone stayed dark.

"What now?" I asked.

The Hubs paced the floor. "We wait."

"But you told that guy we'd be out in twenty minutes," I said. "We need to pack. And figure out where we're going. Can we use the business center to get on the internet?"

"This hotel doesn't have a business center. It prides itself on unplugging."

"For fuck's sake, remind me again why you picked this place?"

"Don't worry. He'll call," the Hubs assured me.

"We'll have to find an internet cafe," I said.

"Have faith, Jen!" the Hubs snapped.

I waited fifteen minutes and the call never came. Finally I stood up from the threadbare couch and said, "That's it. I'm packing my stuff. I suggest you do the same before they charge our card for another night."

The Hubs was stunned. He rarely loses a game of chicken. He'd finally met his match. "I can't believe it," he muttered, tossing his clothes into his suitcase. "What's he going to do with this room tonight? It's never going to rent. He's lost a customer he could have made for life."

I snickered. "Are you coming back to Stockholm some-time soon? He doesn't give a shit about two dumb Americans."

The Hubs wasn't deterred. "What the hell is wrong with that guy?"

"I don't know, but we need to get moving," I said. "Because I'd like to find a hotel room before it gets dark and it gets dark at five o'clock here."

We bundled up our belongings and left our over-priced rundown hotel room. We rode the elevator down to the lobby in silence. When the doors opened, the Hubs said, "Let me just try one more thing." He headed over to the desk, but the guy we'd been dealing with earlier was no longer there. When the Hubs asked where he was, he was told he'd gone on a smoke break.

"That's hard core," I said, shouldering my backpack. "He's made it clear where he stands. Let's go."

We stumbled into the dusk, unsure where we'd go.

"What now?" the Hubs asked. He didn't have much experience traveling and a lot of the logistics had fallen to me. The one thing he'd planned was the hotel we were now leaving. He was lost.

"We need an internet cafe," I said. "We can look for a hotel-finder service."

Back in the early 2000s the internet was a thing, but it wasn't like it is now. AirBnB, Trivago, and all the other travel sites you can think of didn't exist. If you wanted to find a relatively affordable, clean, safe hotel in a foreign city you went to an actual storefront business that helped match you up with available hotel rooms. You could find everything from hostels to homes in the country and everything in between. I'd used these concierge services in many of the countries I'd visited and always had a very good experience, but I needed the internet to find the address for the storefront.

"I saw an internet cafe around the corner," the Hubs said. "Come on."

We found the cafe and I began my search while the Hubs still grumbled. "I am a little stunned that happened."

"It's fine," I said.

"I really thought he'd give in."

"I know," I said.

"Where are we going to stay tonight?" the Hubs asked.

"We'll be fine," I said, digging in my backpack for a pen and paper because I'd found what we needed. "Write down this address."

. . .

A COUPLE HOURS later we were checking into a small boutique hotel in the older part of Stockholm. The hotel had a nautical theme that carried over to the rooms. The room was very small and cozy, but after the suite we'd just left, it felt cramped and dark.

"This is nice," I said.

"Not really," the Hubs grumped.

The Hubs was regretting his decision and I needed to make it better. There is always one thing that will cheer up the Hubs, no matter how blue he is. "Let's get some food."

It worked like a charm and he perked right up. "Where should we go?" he asked.

"I don't know. But when we checked in the owner said he could recommend some place. Let's get dressed and go downstairs and ask him. We can go somewhere fancy since we're saving so much money by staying here."

We got dressed and headed down to speak to Lars, the owner. Lars was a nice, middle-aged man who spoke impeccable English. "What sort of food are you looking for?" he asked.

"I don't know," I said. "What's Sweden famous for?"

"Meatballs," the Hubs joked.

"I like meatballs," I said.

Lars laughed and shook his head. "No!" he said. "You must have *Surströmming*!"

"That's canned herring," I exclaimed. "No, thank you."

"Hang on," the Hubs said. "We could do seafood. We're on the Baltic Sea. There must be good seafood, right, Lars?"

Lars nodded emphatically. "Oh, yes. There is a wonderful seafood restaurant just two blocks from here."

He scribbled an address on a piece of paper. "Tell them Lars sent you and they'll take excellent care of you!"

Looking back now, all I can think is everyone at the seafood restaurant must have hated Lars' guts.

We followed Lars' directions and arrived at a lovely quaint restaurant. We were seated immediately at a romantic table for two. "This is nice," I said.

"Yeah, I guess so," the Hubs said, looking around warily.

"What's the matter now?" I asked, sighing because I already knew. The restaurant wasn't busy enough for the Hubs. He has a theory that if a restaurant is any good, it will be packed. Empty restaurants are a sign of terrible food and/or service.

I was right. "It's too empty," the Hubs said.

"It's early," I reminded him. "We're still jet-lagged so we're eating at the early-bird seating. I'm sure it will start filling up by the time we leave."

"Uh-huh," the Hubs said. "We'll see."

The waiter returned to the table and asked if we were ready to order.

"Do you have any specials?" the Hubs asked. He loves a good special. He thinks those are better than regular menu items.

"Yes, sir, we have lobster ravioli," the waiter said.

"Ooh, that sounds good," I said.

"Do you want to get it?" the Hubs asked.

I don't remember what I ordered that night, but I do remember that I thought it sounded delicious. Too delicious to set aside to order the lobster ravioli. "No, thanks," I said. "But you should get it and give me a bite." We'd been married less than a week and I was already teaching him how marriage worked.

One hour later he'd be teaching me another lesson about how marriage worked.

About halfway through his meal, the Hubs put down his fork and said, "I don't feel so well."

I must admit, I didn't take him very seriously. The Hubs is known for his elaborate man-colds. He can nurse a sniffle for a week. We were both very tired after our wedding and the long flights. We were stressed about our hotel situation and I was sure he was just suffering from a tinge of anxiety. "You'll be fine," I assured him.

"Yeah, probably," he said, taking another bite of his dinner.

You can say many things about the Hubs, but you can't call him a quitter. It doesn't matter how full he feels, The Hubs has never left a plate with food on it and that night was no different. He gulped down every ravioli and slopped up every bit of cream sauce. When I asked for a bite, he snapped, "No! I think the lobster is bad."

"What?" I exclaimed. "Are you serious?"

He took another bite to confirm. "Yeah, I'm pretty sure it's turned," he said, nodding.

"Well, we need to tell the waiter. Stop eating!" I said. I couldn't believe he was forcing himself to eat expired seafood!

The Hubs shook his head. "No," he said. "It'll be fine. I've eaten worse. We ate that horrible Chinese food in Estonia! If that didn't kill me, this won't."

"Yeah, sorry about that Chinese food," I said, grimacing.

While walking through the old town of Tallinn, I'd had the great idea that it would be cool and romantic if we started a tradition on our honeymoon that we'd carry throughout our entire marriage. I imagined that every time we traveled somewhere, we'd do this particular tradition and we'd smile lovingly at one another say, "We started this on our honeymoon and we've done it ever since."

I was sure that someday long after we were gone, our grandchildren would stop themselves and say, "Aww, grandma and grandpa started this on their honeymoon."

When I'd told the Hubs my idea, he said, "Okay, so what should our tradition be?"

That was the problem. I had no idea. I tried to think of other romantic traditions people had. "We could carve our initials into a tree," I suggested.

The Hubs wrinkled his nose. "I don't know about that. It would have to be a decent-size tree. And it might be illegal in some places. Plus, I don't even own a pocketknife."

"How about we renew our vows in every city we visit?"

"Seriously, Jen? You hate people who renew their vows."

I nodded. "I know, I know. Dumb idea."

"What if we bought a magnet everywhere we went?" the Hubs said.

"Huh?"

"A magnet. For our fridge."

"That's not romantic," I argued. "Why not buy a shot glass too?"

"I read an article about a bridge somewhere where you put a lock on the bridge to symbolize your love. We could do that."

"I heard that bridge is collapsing under the weight of the locks and other cities have banned the practice."

"Hmm. That makes sense," the Hubs said, nodding.

"What if we bought a piece of jewelry everywhere we went?"

"How is that different than my magnet idea?"

"Jewelry is romantic."

"Jewelry is expensive," the Hubs said.

We were having this conversation while looking for a place to have lunch. We hadn't found anything that we could agree on when I spotted a familiar-looking sign. I nudged the Hubs, "Look," I said, pointing.

"What am I looking for?"

"See the dragons? The red lanterns? It's a Chinese restaurant. In Estonia. Who would have thought there would be a Chinese restaurant in the Old Town."

The Hubs shrugged. "We're everywhere."

I had an idea. "Hey! What if our tradition is that wherever we go, we always have a romantic dinner together at a Chinese restaurant?"

To this day, I'm not sure what they served us, but it wasn't like any Chinese food either of us had ever had.

"That reminds me," the Hubs said as I recalled strange Chinese food in Estonia. "We need a new tradition." He burped and looked a little green.

"Are you okay?" I asked. He didn't look good and was starting to sweat.

He mopped his brow with his napkin. "Yeah, I think I need some fresh air, though."

"Go outside," I said. "I'll pay the bill."

"Don't complain about the food, Jen," the Hubs said. "I probably just ordered wrong."

I paid the check and stepped outside only to find the Hubs in the alleyway vomiting. "Holy shit!" I said. "What can I do?"

The Hubs was mortified. "Nothing," he rasped. "Stay back. I don't want you to see me like this."

"Let me help you."

He was shaky and let me hold him up as we slowly made our way back to our hotel. Lars was gone so I couldn't tell him that his fabulous restaurant had poisoned my brand new husband.

We got to our room just in time for the Hubs to unload again. "Leave!" he cried. "You can't stay here when I'm like this!"

I couldn't leave him. One, because he was my husband and I'd literally promised just two weeks prior to be there in sickness and in health, and two because it was late and everything was closed. I had nowhere to go.

He slammed the bathroom door shut and stayed in there all night, heaving his guts. I turned on the TV, mostly to drown out the noise, and found reruns of "Frasier" dubbed into Swedish. It was the best I could do.

The Hubs was sick for the next two days. He missed almost all of Stockholm because he forced himself to eat rancid lobster. I knew he was a cheap bastard who hated to let anything go to waste, but I had no idea the lengths he would go!

Looking back now I think it's adorable how he was embarrassed to have me see him throwing up. He thought it might change my perception of him or that I might not find him attractive anymore. Meanwhile, now, after almost twenty years of marriage, vomiting is probably one of the least disgusting things he does in front of me. Shit. Just this week he asked me to pop a pimple between his ass cheeks. I told him I'd rather eat lobster ravioli in Stockholm.

EIGHT

MISCOMMUNICATION: THE STORY OF MY FIRST MASSAGE

SINGAPORE

2003

My parents have traveled all over the world and if you ask them to share their favorite city, they always say, "Singapore."

I didn't know much about Singapore except it was a very long plane ride away and super humid. The idea of possibly suffering from an embolism just so I could go sweat somewhere sounded awful. I didn't need to travel halfway around the world for swampcrotch and frizzy hair. I could be in Florida in two-and-a-half hours! But when my parents offered to take us to Singapore, the Hubs and I didn't hesitate a moment before we said, "Yes!" *Hello, free trip*! I don't think my brother, C.B. and his wife, Ida, balked either. You don't say no to a free trip.

My mom is a huge fan of Christmas and she'd always wanted to celebrate her favorite holiday in Singapore with her family. I know that probably sounds a little weird to you. It sounded weird to me too. Because when I think of celebrating Christmas in a foreign city, my first thought is somewhere snowy and bucolic, like a Hallmark Christmas movie on crack. Maybe Santa Claus Village, Finland, where they have actual reindeer? Or how about Vienna, Austria, where we could hear the Vienna Boys Choir sing on Christmas Eve? Hell, even London does Christmas in style. I had no idea what Christmas in Singapore was like, but again, it was a free trip, so I wasn't going to argue.

It was before any of us had kids, so we could manage a long plane ride and a Christmas without Santa. The flight over was as long and excruciating as you'd imagine. I think I watched four movies and fell asleep only to be woken up by a flight attendant offering me a hot towel and midnight snack. "Are we there yet?" I asked.

"Almost halfway," the flight attendant said.

Jesus.

My mom was seated across the aisle from me. "Tell me again why you like this place so much?" I grumbled.

Mom put down her book and smiled brightly at me. "Oh, Jen! It's a wonderful city," she said. "It's beautiful and so clean."

"Yeah, I read they'll cane me or something if I chew gum," I said.

Her smile faltered a bit. "I think that rule is just for the locals. I've never been stopped for having gum."

"Right."

"And the food! It's delicious! The shopping is incredible! But my favorite part is the spa."

I perked up. I mean, I like food and shopping, but I *really* like pampering. "Go on," I said.

"Your dad and I have a favorite spa that we go to every time we're there. It's so relaxing and the people who work there are just amazing at what they do. I've already made appointments for a girls' day with you, me, and Ida. We'll go the first day we're there. It's my Christmas gift to both of you. You're going to love it."

I dozed off dreaming of incredible foot massages and soothing facials...and the occasional sugar plum fairy.

THE NEXT MORNING I met Mom and Ida in the lobby of the hotel and was surprised to see employees taking down the massive Christmas tree. I had caught a glimpse of the tree when we arrived the night before, but I was too exhausted to take it in properly. I only remember it was quite austere compared to my mother's standards of decorating. "What's going on with the tree?" I asked.

Mom looked sad. "Since it's the day after Christmas, apparently, all the decorations need to come down because New Year's is a bigger celebration and they need to decorate for that."

"Huh," I said. "So much for Christmas in Singapore."

"Yeah," Mom grumbled. "I don't even really like New Year's."

"Yeah, well, that sucks," I said. "But at least we have our spa day!"

Mom instantly brightened. "Yes!" she squealed. "Let's go!"

When we arrived at the spa we were immediately greeted by Jane, the manager. She knew my mom by name.

"How much have you spent here?" I whispered.

"Shh," Mom said before she went in to give Jane a big hug.

"These are your girls?" Jane asked, motioning at me and Ida.

"Yes! I've been so anxious to bring them here and give them the full experience!"

"Of course!" Jane said. "It will be unforgettable."

It's been seventeen years and I haven't forgotten one detail, so I can't say Jane was a liar.

"Where are the boys?" Jane asked, looking past us.

"Oh, they didn't want to do spa stuff. They're doing their own thing today," Mom said.

"Ah, of course," Jane said. She clapped her hands. "Okay. It's time. Come, come, ladies."

Jane led us down a long marble hallway and into a luxurious locker room. She pointed out three wooden lockers and left us.

I'd never had a massage before. The closest I'd come was that guy in the middle of the mall who drapes you over his chair and charges ten bucks for ten minutes to jab you in the back and calls it a massage. So I was way out of my comfort zone. "What do we do?" I asked.

Ida shrugged. She was just as clueless as I was. "This is your mom's party," Ida said.

Mom was already stripping down to her birthday suit. "Whoa, Mom!" I said, throwing a look over my shoulder. The locker room wasn't full, but it wasn't empty either. "Aren't you supposed to go somewhere to do that?"

Mom pulled a fluffy white robe from her locker and wrapped it around her body. "No! That's the best part about this place! No one cares what anyone looks like. Last time, I went to the sauna completely *naked*."

Mom has a tendency to be a bit of a Puritan, so it was shocking to see her so wild and free.

"So, we just..." I looked at Ida who was already pulling off her pants.

"When in Rome," Ida said.

Easy for her to say. Ida was a few months pregnant and even pregnant her body was fantastic. I was super uncomfortable. "Is there a restroom?" I asked.

Mom sighed. "Yes, it's around the corner. Take your robe with you."

I took the robe and ducked into the stall. I shucked my clothes and grabbed the robe off the hanger, but as soon as I put my arms in, I knew there was going to be a problem. I managed to get my shoulders wedged into the robe, but I couldn't close it completely over my ample bosom. It was like putting twenty pounds of dog food into a ten-pound bag.

"Shit," I muttered.

I was just trying to figure out what to do when Mom came into the restroom to check on me. "Everything okay, Jen?"

"The robe is too small. My boobs are hanging out."

"Oh, yeah, I was afraid of that," Mom said. "The robes are snug on me. Everyone in Asia is so much smaller. Let me find Jane and see what she can do."

I waited several minutes before hearing the outer door open and Jane say, "The robe is okay. Your daughter is very big."

Yes, thank you, Jane. I appreciate that.

"Let's just try this one, Jane," Mom said. She knocked on the door to my stall. "Jen? I brought a men's robe. You want to try that?"

I cracked the door a bit and looked at the robe skeptically. It didn't look much bigger than the one I was wearing, but I didn't have a lot of choice at that point. "Yes, okay," I sighed.

"Do you need help?" Mom asked.

"Is she stuck in the robe?" Jane asked.

"No, I'm not stuck," I snapped. "Just give me a second." I worked up a sweat wrestling myself out of the tiny robe. *What the fuck? This was supposed to be a*

*relaxing day and now I'm all pissed off and worried about
everything.*

"Calm down, Jen," Mom said, as if reading my thoughts.
"I can feel you freaking out from here. It's going to be fine."

I took a deep breath and tried to calm myself. "What if
this one doesn't fit?" I asked.

"It's okay. We get you a sheet," said Jane.

Oh, fuck you, Jane.

I shoved my arms in the men's robe and could feel
immediately that it was a more generous cut. *This might
work,* I thought. *Fuck it. I'll make it work.* I was prepared to
shove my tits under my arm-pits if I had to. Luckily, it didn't
come to that. I was able to close the robe and emerged from
the bathroom stall.

"Oh, that looks nice," Mom said.

God bless Mom for always trying to make me feel pretty
even when I know I look hideous. "It's a men's robe, Mom.
Probably made for a sumo wrestler or something." I noticed
that Jane didn't disagree with me.

"Okay, let's go," Mom said. "Ida's already started her
pedicure."

There was a whole agenda for the day. We began with
mani-pedis and then proceeded to facials. After our facials,
we had a break for a delicious lunch and a quick sauna and
plunge in the cool pool before retiring to the meditation
room.

Jane found us in the meditation room. "Ready for
massage?" Jane asked.

"Ooh, my favorite part," Mom said, excitedly. "Let's go,
girls."

We were each escorted to our own private room, which
wasn't that unusual. We'd been in private rooms for our
facials. Ida and I were next door to one another. Ida glanced

at me before disappearing into her chamber. "I guess I'll see ya...later," she said.

"Yup. Bye. Enjoy."

Until that point we'd kept our robes on for all our services. I could tell the naked women around us in the sauna were laughing at the prudish Americans sweating to death in their robes. But I didn't care. I wasn't comfortable being naked. But Mom warned us at lunch, "You'll want to be naked for your massage."

"Really?" I asked, forking a strawberry into my mouth.

"Yes, if you want a good experience, you should be naked. They'll exfoliate your whole body and you'll want the hot stones. All of it. It's really, okay, Jen. You won't feel strange after about five minutes. Just let go and have fun," Mom said.

I sighed, heavily. "Okay, I'll try."

Remembering my promise to my mother, I reluctantly shed my robe and hung it on the hook on the back of the door. I slid under the warm sheets and tried to *let go and have fun.*

There was a soft knock on the door and a tiny Asian woman walked in. "I'm Mary."

"Hello. I'm Jen. I've never done this, so if I act weird, that's why."

Mary giggled. "English, no good."

I frowned. So far everyone in Singapore I'd come into contact with spoke better English than I did. I was surprised Mary couldn't speak English, but I reminded myself I was in a foreign country and it was very elitist of me to assume everyone could communicate with me. "Okay," I said.

"Ready?" Mary asked.

"Ready."

Mary indicated I should be on my stomach to start, so I

rolled over and got myself into position. Mom was right, within five minutes, I'd completely forgotten I was naked and letting a strange woman touch my body. The room was dark and cozy. The music was soothing and mellow. The table was soft and warm. Mary's magic hands worked out every kink and pain I had acquired from the flight over. She rubbed onto my skin some kind of salt scrub and polished the shit out of me. She washed my body and covered me in hot stones over layers of warm oils and creams. It was sheer bliss.

I was half asleep when Mary motioned for me to roll over onto my back. I flipped over and settled into my warm little nest of blankets as she began massaging my neck and shoulders. She did something magical to my head that I've still never had a masseuse repeat. And then she asked, "Okay to do front?"

I was confused. I'd already turned over. She'd been focused on my shoulders for a good ten minutes. What did she mean? I thought of the witchcraft she'd worked on my scalp and I didn't want her to stop, but I also knew her English wasn't great. I didn't care. I was putty in her hands, I figured she could do whatever she wanted. So I said, "Yes, please."

"Okay," Mary said. And then without another word she hoisted a tiny leg up and over my body and in a flash she was sitting on top of me, straddling me. She snatched the warm blankets off my chest and I felt the cool air conditioning on my nipples.

"Oh, god," I squeaked.

"Is good," Mary said pouring a large quantity of oil into her hands. And then she grabbed my left breast and began kneading it like a loaf of fucking bread dough.

"Lord," I cried.

"Is good," Mary said, beaming. She wrung my breast through her hands, squeezing my flesh through her strong fingers like it was a ball of clay she needed to mold into a goddamn pot.

"Jesus," I whimpered.

"Is good," Mary said, nodding and smiling. She looked right into my eyes as she pinched the fuck out of my nipple.

"Ow!" I exclaimed.

Mary slapped my breast back and forth between her hands like she was tenderizing a raw fucking steak.

I was young and shy back then. I wasn't the feisty broad I am now, so I didn't know what to do. I didn't feel violated in any way. What Mary was doing to me was incredibly professional, it was just unusual. I felt like Mom had prepared me for what to expect and yet, she failed to mention this part!

Mary wrung my breast like it was a wet dishtowel and then dropped it triumphantly before she turned her attention to my right breast.

"Oh, shit," I whispered. "It's only half done."

I was reminded of the dentist, which I hate. In both cases, they're just doing their job and I'm feeling massively uncomfortable. And then, just like the drill, it was over. Mary climbed off and wiped her greasy hands on a towel. "Is okay?" she asked.

"Yes," I said, closing my eyes. It was too hard to make eye contact with Mary after we'd been so...intimate...and yet incredibly professional...with one another.

Mary left me alone to wriggle back into my man-robe and disposable flip flops. I must have looked a little shell-shocked when I emerged from my room because Ida immediately grabbed my arm and asked, "Are you okay?"

"Yes," I mumbled. "I'm fine."

It was teatime, so we walked in silence back to the lounge and found Mom devouring cookies. "These are my favorites," she said, spitting cookie crumbs at me. "Try them!"

Normally, I never say no to cookies, but I was still reeling a bit from my massage, so I collapsed into the seat next to her. Ida sat down beside me.

"So? How was it, girls?" Mom asked. "*Ah-may-zing,* right?"

Ida and I exchanged a look and suddenly I realized she'd had the same experience. "Did you...did you say yes to the...front?" I whispered.

Ida's eyes grew wide. "I did. Did you?"

I nodded solemnly. "I did."

"Did she...massage your..."

"She mashed them like potatoes at Christmas," I said.

Ida nodded. "Yeah," she said. "Same here."

Mom stopped eating her cookies. "What are you two whispering about over there? Did you not have a good service? I can talk to Jane. What's the matter?"

Ida looked at me, pleading. She was the outsider here, the one who married into my wackadoo family. She couldn't start this conversation. I had to be the one to talk to Mom. I turned in my seat and faced Mom squarely. "Mom, why didn't you warn us that massages here are different than at home?"

Mom frowned. "What are you talking about? You don't even know what a massage at home is like."

"Well, I think I understand the basics, Mom, and I don't think breasts are typically on the menu."

Mom choked on her cookie. "What? Breasts? What are you talking about?"

"You should have warned us," I repeated.

"Warned you about what?" Mom asked.

"About...the *boob* thing..." I said.

"The boob thing? What boob thing?" Mom asked. I could see she was genuinely confused.

I looked back at Ida. She shook her head. I was on my own. "Mom, the masseuse straddled us and massaged our boobs."

"I didn't get straddled," Ida said. "Maybe because I told her I was pregnant."

"What?" Mom screeched. "What are you talking about?"

I quickly filled in Mom on the whole pulping of the breasts. Ida threw in a few choice details from her experience too.

"Oh my god," Mom said.

"I kept saying that, but the lady thought I was just being a good Christian or something," I said.

"So you're telling me, the girl climbed on top of you and..."

"Pounded the shit out of my breasts, yes."

"So she *touched* you?" Mom whispered, scandalized.

"No! It was not like that," I assured her. "There was nothing sexual about it. Her grip was all business. There was clearly a language barrier between us and I have proven time and time again today that I'm an uptight Puritanical American."

"So, what did you do?" Mom asked.

"Nothing! I just laid there and pretended it was just like getting a mammogram and willed myself not to get turned on," I said.

Ida nodded. Mom was quiet for a minute. Finally, she spoke. "Well, I'm shocked to hear this," she said. "I've been coming here for years. Jane is like a friend to me."

"I know," I said, nervously. I was a bit worried Mom was going to get mad at Jane and Mary, but I really felt like it was a cultural thing. Mary asked me if I was okay and I said I was. I just didn't understand what was going to happen. I opened my mouth to try and explain all of this to Mom but she cut me off.

"Why do you think they've never tried to touch my breasts?" Mom asked, her eyes narrowing.

"Um...I don't know," I said. I shot a glance at Ida but she was focused on the cookies.

"I think it's odd that I've been coming here for years and not once did anyone try and massage *my* breasts. She got a petulant look on her face.

I grimaced. *Oh fuck. Where's she going with this?*

"Why did they do that to you two?" she asked. I could hear the bitterness creeping into her voice. "Are my breasts *too old*?"

I gagged a bit. "Mom..."

She waved her hand at me. "No, it's fine. I didn't want that sort of treatment anyway." She stuffed a cookie in her mouth.

When we were changing back into clothes later that day I saw an American woman in the locker room. She looked as out of sorts as I had a few hours earlier. But I was wiser now. I'd seen some shit and I couldn't let her go down the same path I did—unless she wanted to, of course. So, when I saw her washing her hands at the sinks, I hurried over to join her.

"First time here?" I asked, casually.

"Yes," she said, excited.

"You're getting a massage?"

"Yes," she said, drying her hands.

"Cool," I said. "Listen, if they ask you if want the front done, they mean the whole front. Like, *the whole thing.*"

The woman stared at me like I had two heads. I used my hands to pretend I was cupping my own breasts. "*All* of it," I said. "The whole shebang."

I could see she was still not understanding what I was trying to tell her.

I leaned in and whispered, "If you say yes, they will man-handle and pulverize the shit out of your breasts like they're making sausage."

"Oh Jesus," she gasped, finally getting it.

I nodded. "Is good," I said.

NINE

MOMS GET SH*T DONE

SAN DIEGO, CALIFORNIA

2009

The Hubs and I used to think nothing of jumping in the car with an overnight bag and heading off toward the horizon with only the Universe guiding us. But then we had kids.

Travel changed drastically. Children don't do well with the kind of spontaneous travel the Universe provides. I now had to think about where the kids would sleep best because there's nothing worse than vacationing with an over-tired child. I had to pack enough snacks, toys, books, and sippy cups to keep them happy because toddler meltdowns on airplanes are an actual circle of hell. I had to double and triple check the weather to make sure I had enough layers to keep their little bodies warm or cool. I had to pick hotels based solely on whether or not they had an indoor pool.

We decided that the way to make our kids good travelers was to start them early. We took Gomer on his first airplane ride just before his first birthday. He sat on my lap the entire way, staring at the interactive map on the screen in front of him while sucking down one bottle after another.

We were flying to New York City to see the Hubs' family. Since it was our first time traveling with a child, we didn't think long and hard enough about the sleeping conditions. We just booked a normal hotel room and requested a crib. When we arrived we found the tiniest shoebox room I've ever seen. The queen-sized bed sat in the middle of the room, a small crib wedged between the end of the bed and the wall. There was no other place where the crib would fit, but with it there, there was no room to walk around the bed. We had to climb over the bed to get to the other side of the room.

Because Gomer was still an only child, he was used to going to sleep in a very quiet house. At home, when his bedtime rolled around, we'd turn down all the lights and limit the noise in the house. Once Gomer was in bed, the Hubs and I would go all the way to the basement so the noise from our television didn't disturb him while he slumbered two floors above us.

That first night in New York we put Gomer in his crib and then sort of looked at each other.

"What do we do now?" the Hubs whispered.

"Hmm, good question," I whispered.

Gomer laid stiffly in his unfamiliar bed, his enormous eyes staring at us through the slats in the crib.

"Can we watch TV?" the Hubs asked.

The television was mounted on the wall above Gomer's head. "No, he'll never settle down if we do," I said.

"What are we going to do all night?" the Hubs complained. "It's only six-thirty."

Gomer stood up in his bed and shouted, "Up! Up! Up!" He shook the flimsy sides and demanded to be released from his prison.

"Shh," I said. "Go to sleep, Gomer." I laid him back down and covered him with his blanket.

He immediately started fussing and I could tell he wasn't going to go to sleep with us staring at him.

"We need to leave him alone," I said.

The Hubs looked around the tiny room. "Where would you like us to go?" he asked.

Besides a small closet, there was only one place to escape. "It's going to have to be the bathroom," I said.

We turned off all the lights in the room and left Gomer alone while we moved into the bathroom. I took my book and climbed into the tub and stretched out. The Hubs frowned. "So I guess I get the toilet?" he asked.

"You're too long for the tub. This isn't as comfortable as it looks, you know."

"Right," the Hubs scoffed. He perched his bony ass on the toilet and stared at me.

I looked up from my book. "What?"

"I don't have anything to do," he whined. The Hubs never travels with a book.

I sighed. "Stay here," I ordered.

I crawled out of the bathroom practically on my belly so Gomer wouldn't see me. I could hear him babbling to himself. I got to the bedside table and groped around blindly until I found what I was looking for. I returned to the bathroom with the local shopping and dining guides the hotel provided for each room. "Here," I said, tossing the glossy publications in the Hubs' lap. "These will have to do."

That night we decided we'd never travel again without booking at least two rooms.

We didn't need to worry, though, because within a year Adolpha was born, and she was an absolute terror to live with let alone travel with, so all travel was put on hold.

I think the first trip we took with both kids was to San

Diego. We'd learned our lesson from New York and this time we booked one of those all-suites hotels so we wouldn't have to camp out in the bathroom again.

The morning we left our house for the airport Gomer and I had a fight. He was three years old and still not potty-trained. At his most recent check-up, his pediatrician had lectured me about pressuring him.

"No one goes off to kindergarten in a diaper," he reassured me. "But they do get anxiety from parental pressures. He'll do it when he's ready."

I heard what the doctor said, but I really didn't believe him. I had a good friend who was a kindergarten teacher and she told me all kinds of things her students couldn't do, including pee in the toilet. Plus, by that point I was paying for and changing diapers on two kids and I needed a break.

I'd been on Gomer for weeks to grow up and get out of diapers, so imagine my surprise when he decided *that* morning was the morning he'd do it.

I was trying to wrestle him into a diaper when he announced, "Big boy pants!"

Oh for fuck's sake, I thought. *Now you want to train yourself?*

"Gomer, I'm so happy you're ready for big boy pants," I said. "Let's do that when we get back from our vacation, okay?" We'd be on airplanes or in airports for the next few days. We were going to be in a rental car stuck in southern California traffic for hours at a time. We were planning on going to Legoland and other all-day excursions. The last thing I wanted to do was try and find clean public bathrooms for a toddler on the verge of pissing his pants.

"No!" he insisted. "I'm big boy now!"

I glanced at the clock. We were running out of time and we needed to get to the airport early enough to check car seats, a stroller, blankets, lovies, toys, and everything else but the goddamn kitchen sink.

"Okay, okay," I said. "How about Lightning McQueen?" I pulled out the unopened box of Pull-Ups I'd been trying to get Gomer to wear for weeks. I figured the Pull-Ups would give me a little leeway in case he couldn't hold it long enough to find a restroom.

Gomer shook his head emphatically. "No! Big. Boy. Pants."

Oh, shit. He wanted real fucking underwear. And just like that, my mental packing list tripled.

The Hubs stuck his head in the doorway. "Everyone good in here? I'm loading the car, making sure we have everything."

"I need another suitcase out of storage," I said.

"What? Why?"

"Because your son has decided today is the day he will wear underwear. We all know there will be accidents, so I will need to pack him more clothes."

"Oh, shit," the Hubs said. "Today? Really? You're going to let him do that, Jen?"

"There's no letting or not letting him. He's determined to do it."

The Hubs brought me another suitcase and I threw extra clothes in it, hoping I had enough. "You know there are Targets in San Diego," the Hubs reminded me.

A FEW HOURS later we were on the plane and winging our way to sunny California. I was seated between Adolpha and Gomer, holding a portable DVD player so they could watch a movie and eat their weight in Goldfish crackers. I like my children to be quiet when we travel and the best ways to keep them quiet are: endless screen time, copious snacks, and a fuck ton to drink. My number one mistake was I hadn't revised my general strategy even though it was Gomer's first attempt to go anywhere without his diaper safety net.

Gomer put down his baggie of Goldfish and whined, "Mommy, I have to go potty." He immediately started wiggling in his seat. "I need my special seat."

"Oh! Okay!" I jumped into action. Gomer's "special seat" was a foldable potty seat insert. I didn't even know such a thing existed until a friend handed hers down to me. Her son was over four years old when he finally potty-trained and part of the delay was that he was terrified he'd fall into the toilet.

"You have all your house toilets fitted and ready to go, but it's the damn public toilets that will fuck everything up for you," she explained when she handed over the cherished potty-seat.

"Mommy," Gomer whined. "Hurry. I need to go bad."

"Okay, buddy," I said, digging through all my carry-on bags. "I'm trying to find your special seat. You want it, right?"

"Yes," Gomer said, tugging on the front of his pants.

"Here it is!" I said, waving the little potty seat in the air. "Let's go!"

I quickly unbuckled us and stepped over Adolpha and into the aisle. I was reaching back over her to grab Gomer when the flight attendant made a beeline straight to me. "Ma'am," she said. "Ma'am! You need to return to your seat, please."

"I just need to take my son to the bathroom," I said, hoisting Gomer over Adolpha's legs and into the aisle with me.

"It's too late," the flight attendant said. "We've already begun our descent."

"We have?" I asked. "I didn't hear the announcement."

"Well, the captain just announced it. You need to remain in your seats."

Gomer was literally dancing in the aisle. "I can't do that," I said. "He's just learning how to use the bathroom. He can't hold it. I even have a special seat." I waved my seat in her face as if that might convince her of the severity of our situation.

She looked disgusted. "You should have taken him before we began our descent. It's FAA rules."

"Look at him," I argued. "He needs to go. He'll be done in thirty seconds. We'll be back in our seats before you know it."

"I can't allow you to go to the bathroom," she said, blocking the aisle.

"Oh come on, lady," the woman in the aisle seat behind me said. "She could have been done by now if you'd just let her go."

The flight attendant glared at the woman. "I'm just doing my job."

I couldn't argue with that, but did she need to do her job so well?

"How long until we land?" I asked.

"About thirty minutes," the flight attendant said.

"Thirty minutes! Oh my god! He can't wait that long!" I said. "This is an emergency."

Gomer started crying. "Mommy," he wailed. "I'm need to go potty!"

"He's just a little kid!" Now it was the woman seated in front of me arguing on my behalf. Women supporting women is my fucking love language.

"Yes!" the flight attendant said. "All the more reason to take precautions. We are descending. He could be seriously injured."

"I'll take full responsibility," I said.

"I cannot allow it," she said. "Please take your seat."

"Or what?" the first woman asked.

The flight attendant glared at her but didn't say anything. Because, yeah, what could she really do if I shoved past her with Gomer under my arm like a football? Land the plane? We were already landing! Arrest me? I didn't have my huge social media platform yet, but even the puny following I did have could make that story go viral.

I didn't know what to do. Believe it or not I am a rule follower. I didn't want to get arrested by air marshals! But Gomer was practically turning blue from holding his breath and his pee for so long. He was trying so hard not to ruin his fancy Jack Sparrow underwear and there was nothing I could do. I was furious with the flight attendant. I knew she was following the rules too, but it felt like I was dealing with a robot instead of a human being. How could she look at my suffering kid and not be moved by his plight? And she had wasted so much precious time arguing with me instead of just saying, "Make it quick, Mama!"

"Fine," I said. "But it will be your mess to clean up."

"Excuse me?" the flight attendant said.

I turned to Gomer. "Go ahead, Gomer. Go potty."

"Mommy!" He was shocked. "I can't. I'll make the carpet all wet."

"That is true," I said. "But it's okay. Just this one time."

"Ma'am," the flight attendant sputtered. "He cannot do that."

"I wish there was another way," I said. "But you've left me no choice."

"Ma'am!"

"Mommy!" Gomer cried. "My pants will get all wet. I'll have wet pants!"

That was true. It wasn't Gomer's fault that we couldn't use the restroom. He shouldn't be punished by walking around in wet pants.

"Okay, let's not get your pants wet, then," I said. I pulled on the elastic waistband of his shorts and he practically screamed.

"Mommy! No! I can't have my peepee out! It's inappropriate."

Damn the Hubs and I for working so hard on him about appropriate and inappropriate times to show off his junk.

Suddenly, a brilliant idea popped into my head. I reached over Adolpha and dug in my bag again until I found what I was looking for. I pulled out an empty sippy cup—probably the exact sippy cup that had put us into this predicament. I unscrewed the lid and held it out to Gomer. "Just pee in here," I instructed.

Gomer was horrified. "Noooo," he wailed. "Noooo!"

I could see from his dance moves that we were running out of time. It was either pee in the empty sippy cup or pee his pants.

"It will be okay," I promised. "Totally appropriate and no wet pants. Trust me, buddy." The good thing about boys is they can literally pee anywhere and into anything—including an empty sippy cup. A few quick moves and I had Gomer in position but still very private. As soon as the cool breeze hit his bare skin, he was a goner. His bladder couldn't take another second and I felt his whole body relax and kind of lean against me. He was still mortified, but also relieved.

"Mommy," he whimpered, totally ashamed.

"It's okay, buddy," I whispered. "You're doing great."

I could feel the cup starting to get heavy. I knew it was almost full. I prayed it wouldn't overflow. But just in case it did, I moved us a hair so the flight attendant's shoes were in the splash zone.

I felt Gomer's weight shift as he quickly fixed his pants. "All good?" I asked.

"Yes," he sighed.

I gave him a kiss on the top of his head. "Great job, Gomer. I'm so proud of you for being such a big boy and going potty for the *first* time. Go back to your seat, please."

I checked the sippy cup it was full to the brim. I quickly screwed on the cap.

"Did he pee in the cup?" the woman in front of me asked. "Or on the floor?"

"The cup," I replied.

"Nice," she said, giving me a thumbs up.

The flight attendant looked a little green. "Do you want to throw that out?" she asked, pointing at the sippy cup of pee in my hand.

The woman across the aisle laughed loudly. "Hell no, that's a good sippy cup!"

"No way," I said. "I'll wash it. It's just pee. It's been puked in before too."

The flight attendant looked even queasier. "I can't believe you did that," she said.

I shrugged. "Moms get shit done," I said.

Every woman within earshot applauded.

TEN

I TOLD YOU ALREADY: MOMS GET SH*T DONE.

NEW YORK CITY

2010

We'd had a long, fun visit with family and friends in New York City and it was time to return to Kansas City, but when we arrived at the airport, we discovered our flight was delayed due to a mechanical problem. Everyone in the gate area groaned and began demanding to know when the plane could fly. "It could be half an hour, or it could be four hours," the man behind the counter said. "We really don't know."

"I'm going to try and figure out if there's a way out of here," the Hubs said.

That meant I was stuck entertaining two tired kids in a crowded airport. But I am the mom who is always prepared. My carry-on bag weighs a fuck ton (just ask my chiropractor) because it's always full of snacks, cups, change of clothes, toys, books, electronic devices, headphones, extra chargers, Wet Wipes, and even a deflated beach ball that I can blow up in a hot minute to distract bored, grumpy kids.

I pulled out a nylon sheet that I carried so the kids could have a clean spot to sit and play. I set them up in a corner near the windows so they could watch planes take off and land if Dora became too obnoxious. The Hubs returned with bad news, "There are no other flights. We have to wait for this one." So, for the next few hours I plied the kids with unlimited screen time and tons of food.

Suddenly, there was a flurry of activity by the gangway. A guy in coveralls was at the door and giving the thumbs up to the man behind the counter. The man grabbed his microphone and announced, "All right, ladies and gentlemen, it appears it's your time to go. We've got a brief window to get you out of here so you're not delayed on the tarmac, so I'm going to load this plane fast and furious."

While everyone clapped, I threw all of the kids' shit back into my bag. Because we were traveling with small children, I knew we'd be among the first allowed to board and I wanted to be ready. I threw everything into the bag with wild abandon, just needing it hauled onto the plane. I could fix it later. The Hubs pitched in and between the two of us, we had our space cleaned up in thirty seconds. "Let's go," he said, grabbing Adolpha and heading to the line that was already forming. Gomer and I stayed close on his heels. I never looked back. I always look back to make sure we don't forget anything, but that night I didn't look back. I just wanted to get on the plane and go home.

The gate agent wasn't lying, as soon as we hit the line, it started moving and we were in our seats in a flash. I was getting the kids settled in and making sure they had their seatbelts fastened, more fucking snacks, and fully charged devices. That's when I saw that Adolpha didn't have NuNu and Puppy.

NuNu and Puppy aren't real people, but they're as important as real people. NuNu was a ratty pink blanket Adolpha carried everywhere and Puppy was her favorite stuffed animal. These two items were so important to

Adolpha that she couldn't sleep without them. Occasionally Puppy would go missing in our house and it would be cause for a meltdown of epic proportions.

"Where's Puppy?" I asked.

No one answered me. Both kids were enthralled with the cartoons they were watching. The Hubs already had headphones on and was closing his eyes like he might take a nap. I swatted his arm. "What?" he grumbled.

"Where's Puppy and NuNu?" I asked, digging frantically through the bag. "Where did you put them?"

"I didn't pick them up, you did," he said.

"No. I didn't. I would remember where I put them if I picked them up."

"Then, I'm sure they're in there," he said, closing his eyes.

Motherfucker.

"Oh my god, look in your bag, please. We need to find them now!"

The Hubs sighed loudly but bent over to check his bag. "I don't have them," he said. He motioned for my bag. "Here, let me look. You're just not seeing them."

I handed him the bag. I grabbed Adolpha's tiny backpack that was really only big enough to hold a baggie of Cheerios and a sippy cup, but I hoped Puppy and NuNu were somehow in there.

"Hey!" she griped. "My bag!"

"I know, I know," I said. "Are Puppy and NuNu in there?" I hesitated to tell her they were missing. There's a *Twilight Zone* episode where all of the adults are afraid of the little kid because if you make him angry, he'll turn you into a jack-in-the-box and wish you into the cornfield. That's what toddler Adolpha was like. We walked on eggshells.

"No, they're in the window," Adolpha said, pointing to the airplane window.

"What?" There was no way a stuffed animal and a blanket were in the airplane window.

"They wanted to watch me fly," she said.

Realization dawned on me. They weren't in the plane window. They were in the airport window. Oh.

My.

God.

"You left them in the airport?" I asked.

She nodded proudly. "Yes, we'll get them when we come back later."

Fuuuuuuuck!!!

I quickly calculated the time. We'd been on the plane for a few minutes and the gate agent had said we were going to go fast. The pilot had already announced he was going to fly the plane like he stole it. I had no idea how long I had, but I had to go get Puppy and NuNu or I'd be sent to The Dark Place.

I jumped out of my seat.

"Jen!" the Hubs yelled. "Where are you going?"

But I didn't have time to stop and explain, I had to go! The aisle was completely jammed with people boarding. I threaded myself through the river of passengers like a salmon swimming upstream. Now, I am not a small woman and I'm sure we've all been on a plane before, so we're familiar with how narrow the aisle is, but that day I was like water. I "ope'd" like a good Midwestern and "scootched by." I slithered around and through groups of people. I even stepped on an armrest at one point and did the most awkward parkour anyone has ever seen. When I made it to the front of the plane a very stern looking flight attendant blocked my path. "Where do you think you're going?" she demanded. She was standing between me and the open door.

"I need out," I said.

"Why?" She glared at me. "We're taking off in about five minutes."

I frowned. Five minutes was better than two minutes, I figured. I wasn't a fast runner, but I could do it. I *had* to do it. But first, I was going to waste precious minutes explaining my predicament to this woman. I took a deep breath and exclaimed, "Little girl. Favorite stuffed animal and blankie. Left in the gate area. Must have. No sleep. No peace without."

Instantly, her face softened. We exchanged what can only be described as the international head nod like-minded moms give one another at moments of mutual recognition. I knew immediately that this woman had children and understood exactly what was happening and how dire the situation was. "Go with God," she said, pushing aside a passenger so I could squeeze out the door.

Another woman who had heard the whole thing yelled, "Run like the wind, Mama!"

And I did.

I was the Flash. I was Usain Bolt. I apparated like Hermione fucking Granger. (Harry Potter never passed his test and wasn't very good at it, but Hermione was a genius.)

I dashed up the gangplank, dodging people and roller bags. I flew out the security door and into the gate area. The gate agent was stunned to see me. "Ma'am!" he exclaimed.

But I didn't have time to stop. The last person was almost on the plane already. The gate agent followed me. He didn't run or anything, he was as out of shape as me, but he did a very fast walk. It was like one of those rom-coms where one of the main characters dashes through an airport with security trailing behind but they can't stop because they must tell their one true love about the one true love thing as if telephones don't exist or something. Only my one true love was my daughter and I had to g et her lovies back or there would be hell to pay.

I looked around the gate area but couldn't see Adolpha's stuff. But then I remembered she said she left them in the window. I bolted to the windows and there, tucked behind a partition, were Puppy and NuNu. I tried not to think about the dusty, roach-infested area where Adolpha had tucked her most treasured items. I didn't have time to be grossed out. I snatched her things, turned and ran back to the door that was just starting to close. "Wait!!!" I screamed. "I'm here, I'm here!" NuNu flew behind me like a cape and I held Puppy over my head like a trophy.

The gate agent scowled at me. He wasn't a mom. He didn't get it. "You're not supposed to leave a plane once you've already loaded," he said.

"Sorry," I gasped. "It was an emergency."

He rolled his eyes. "Hurry up, they're waiting for you."

I trotted down to the plane where the flight attendant was waiting for me with a big smile. "You made it," she said.

I was too out of breath to reply. All that running was finally catching up to me.

The plane was fully loaded and I felt like everyone was staring at me as I walked through the aisle with a dingy pink blanket and a floppy dog stuffed under my arm. Some people were giving me a thumbs up and others were irritated I'd delayed them another thirty seconds. *Oh, fuck you, too.*

I found my seat and had barely clicked my seatbelt before we took off. I turned to Adolpha and said, "Hey sweetie, Mommy found Puppy and NuNu! Yay. Would you like to cuddle with them on the way home?"

Adolpha looked up from her screen and smiled at me and said, "No thank you, I'm taking a break from them right now."

Cool, cool, cool. Being a mom is awesome.

ELEVEN

I'M NOT AN IDIOT! I KNOW THE DIFFERENCE BETWEEN A TURTLE AND A SHARK!

KONA, HAWAII

2015

The Hubs and I are both self-employed, so we always forget about vacations. I don't mean we forget to take vacations. We always take vacations! What I mean is, we forget to schedule our vacations. We forget that people with real jobs have to actually plan those. We have no bosses and can work from anywhere, so planning is voluntary.

When our kids were small, we'd just decide on a whim to go somewhere, but that changed once they started school full-time. Apparently, the school district frowns on kids missing a week of school just because Carnival Cruises was having an insane sale. I figured if the homeschooled kids around my town could show up at my garage sales and call it a "math lesson" then surely going on a cruise counted as a "science lesson" or some shit.

Because we're poor planners and only read about a third of the emails the school sends home, school breaks would always sneak up and surprise us. We'd scramble to try and plan a fun trip a week or two before only to find out every single hotel room except the Presidential Suite at two grand a night was booked.

Spring break was always the worst. I can't tell you how many times we waited too long to plan something only to discover that all the good destinations were sold out, so we'd find ourselves driving to St. Louis again.

After three trips in a row to see the Gateway Arch and the Mighty Mississippi, we were so desperate for a real vacation that I actually agreed to listen to a timeshare presentation. A telemarketer offered me a free weekend in New York City in exchange for just one hour of my time to hear about the magic of timeshares. I booked the trip without even talking to the Hubs. I just wanted to go to New York City and have a nice trip with him. I figured we'd plaster fake smiles on our faces and repeat the words, "No, thank you" a million times for sixty minutes and then go see a Broadway show.

I was completely wrong. The Hubs hates Broadway shows and apparently loves the idea of timeshares. We bought a fucking timeshare that weekend.

Now, I can hear many of you groaning right now. "Noooo! A timeshare is a terrible investment, Jen! You'll never use it."

I hear you. I've heard all of the cons of timeshare ownership, but for us, it was exactly what we needed. Now that we've essentially pre-paid our vacations, we won't miss them because the Hubs is a cheap bastard. Now when spring break rolls around and we've forgotten to book a trip, we can check the airfare and see who has the cheapest flights to any of our properties around the world because they always have a place for us.

Because we get a condominium instead of a hotel room, we have room to bring guests with us. Like a few years ago when my parents found out we were going to Hawaii and they invited themselves along. "We can help babysit," Mom promised. Meanwhile, my kids were 9 and 11, so there wasn't a whole lot of babysitting that needed to be done.

My dad didn't like the idea of my brother C.B. and his family being left out, so he asked them to join us as well.

C.B. was happy to go. "But I'll get my own place," he said.

I wanted to say, "Take Mom and Dad with you."

Even though C.B. and his family got their own condominium, we'd get together each day to hang out, play, eat, that sort of thing.

My brother and I are incredibly different in many ways, especially when it comes to his love of the beach. As I've mentioned before, I don't really enjoy the beach, so I enjoy the resort. I want to lounge under an umbrella by the pool and sip cold drinks while I read my book. C.B. always packs his own boogie board and flippers when he travels. I pack giant hats and plenty of caftans. C.B. did a ton of research before we arrived to figure out what beach was the absolute best for the outdoor adventures he had planned for himself and his kids. I knew where the pool with the water slides was.

At dinner one night C.B. told us that the best beach was right down the road and he intended to go the next day. After he enthralled my kids with his stories about catching big waves and feeling like he was flying in the surf, they were hooked, and begged to go with him.

"It's up to your mom," he said. "She needs to come too. I'll have my own two kids to watch. I can't be in charge of all four of you."

I turned to my mom. "Hey, you offered to babysit. Tomorrow would be great," I said.

Mom held up her hands in protest. "Oh no, I'm happy to stay in at night with them, but the doctor wants me to be careful of skin cancer. You know it runs in our family and I had that suspicious mole last year."

Meanwhile, my mother had spent every day of our trip thus far basking in the sun without a care in the world about "suspicious moles."

I looked at the Hubs. "I'll go for the snorkeling, but you know I'm useless in an emergency situation," he said. The Hubs is not the strongest swimmer, especially in the ocean, and I don't like to send my kids anywhere near water with him in charge.

My children coaxed and cajoled me all evening and wore me down until I saw the relaxing day I had planned go *Poof!*

THE NEXT MORNING I packed my biggest hat and a long sleeved t-shirt and traipsed to the local Costco where we bought the kids their own boogie boards so they could keep up with their uncle.

We got to the beach early enough that I could set myself in the only shade I could find. I was crouched under a small, scraggly tree several yards from the ocean. I felt okay, though, because there was a lifeguard station very close and I felt fairly confident they were paying attention.

I spread out my blanket and tried to relax in the perfect Hawaiian day. The sky was bright blue, the sun warm but not hot, and just when I'd start to get a little overheated a breeze would cool me off. The waves were spectacular that day and the beach became quite crowded over the next hour or two. Adults and kids were boogie boarding, snorkeling, body surfing, or just bobbing and floating in the water. Kids were building sandcastles and digging holes. There was even a couple playing Frisbee with a dog. There was so much good people-watching to do I'd sometimes lose sight of my kids. When I couldn't see them I'd leave my shadowy retreat and move closer to the water so I could call them to come back toward to the shore.

After a while, Adolpha had given up trying to boogie board and was building sandcastles, but Gomer was still out there hanging ten, or whatever you call it. He'd gotten too far out and I was wading in the water, trying to call him to come in closer when he caught a wave. The wave crested and he screamed with joy as he rode it toward the shoreline. I stopped yelling and watched my son's face light up. For a moment I was so grateful that we'd been able to bring our kids to this paradise. I was so glad my brother and kids had nagged me to come to the beach with them. I was thrilled to see my child having such an amazingly fun and awesome experience. I was like goddamn Pollyanna standing there on that beach counting my blessings and shit. And that's when I saw the shark.

"What the fuck is that?" I said. I didn't have my glasses on and between the distance and the glare from the sun, I couldn't be sure what I was seeing. I moved deeper into the water toward Gomer so I could see better.

Sure enough, there was a dark mass writhing in the wave just beneath my son. My heart stopped and my feet became lead bricks. I couldn't move. I couldn't make a sound. I just watched the shark glide through the water about a foot below Gomer. It felt like I was frozen for an hour, but it was really just a split second. Suddenly, my feet lightened and air filled my lungs. Just when I was ready to scream, the dark mass was gone and Gomer was landing safely on the beach.

I ran over to him and grabbed him. I didn't want to scare

him, but I also didn't want him to go back out there again. "Are you okay?" I asked, checking him over.

He grimaced. "Yes, mom. I'm fine." He wriggled out of my grip. I knew I was embarrassing him, but I couldn't help myself.

"Did you see that?" I asked. I meant the shark.

Gomer replied, "Yes, it was so cool!" He meant the ride.

My brother washed up on shore next to me, grinning ear to ear. "That was an awesome wave, Gomer!" he yelled.

"Yeah!" Gomer agreed. "I'm going back out!" And before I could snatch him, he turned and ran into the water.

My brother tried to follow, but I clutched at his arm. "C.B.!" I said. "There's a shark out there. I saw it. It was in the same wave Gomer was riding."

C.B. laughed and shook me off. "Jen, there's not a shark out there."

"There is! I saw it. But then it was gone."

"You probably saw a sea turtle, Jen. There are a ton of them out there," C.B. said, rolling his eyes. C.B. is my younger brother, but he's always been known as the "brains" of the family. Even after almost forty years, he has the most irritating way of making me feel stupid sometimes. That was one of those times.

"I think I know the difference between a sea turtle and a shark," I said, exasperated. "I have been to the zoo before."

"Do you, though?" C.B. asked. "Because I'm the one in the water and you're the one buried under an umbrella that's passing as a hat and sitting so far away from the water you're practically in the parking lot. I think I'd notice a shark. I'm always looking for sharks."

I glared. It was one thing to question my eyesight and intelligence, but how dare he attack my hat. My hat was fucking amazeballs. True, it was a bit large, but Mom was right, skin cancer does run in our family and someday he'd be sorry he didn't wear a ridiculously large hat at the beach. "I saw a fin," I stated.

Now, let me be clear here: I was lying. I didn't see a fin, but I said I did because I could tell C.B. didn't believe me. I knew he thought I was being an irrational worrier. He thought my over-active imagination was making me see things and I wasn't. I knew what a fucking turtle looked like and it didn't look like a shark. So, I said I saw a fin, because I figured no one can argue with a fucking fin.

"You saw a fin?" C.B. asked, his eyes narrowing. After spending a lifetime as my little brother he was used to me and my embellishments.

I withered a bit under his gaze. "I think so…" I said.

My brother is an attorney, so he always closes every loophole. "You saw a *shark* fin?"

"Umm…" I said, wavering.

"You probably saw a sea turtle's *flipper*. Look." C.B. pointed. And sure enough an enormous sea turtle was rolling around inside the wave Gomer was riding. "That's what you saw."

I squinted and tried to imagine how a round, friendly, happy turtle could look like a sleek, hungry, killer shark. I couldn't see it, but C.B. had caught me in my lie and I was starting to second-guess my own eyes. I couldn't argue anymore. "Yeah, maybe," I sighed. "You're sure it was a turtle?"

"Positive. There was a dolphin earlier. But there aren't any sharks out there. Besides, the lifeguards are watching, Jen. I think *they'd* see a shark before *you* would." He ran back into the water and left me standing there nervously scanning the water for a dorsal fin. Another sea turtle rolled by, somersaulting in the surf. It looked nothing like what I'd seen.

Fuck, C.B., I thought. *I saw what I saw. There's a shark out there.*

The Hubs waded out of the water to check on me. "You're out of your cave. Everything okay?" he asked, shaking water out of his snorkel.

"I thought I saw a shark," I said.

The Hubs stopped shaking his snorkel. "Really?" he asked, looking out over the water. One thing the Hubs and I have in common is a healthy fear of sharks. "Where?"

"Near the rocks over there. I saw it in the wave Gomer was riding earlier."

"Whoa. For real? Are you sure it was a shark?"

I shrugged. "I thought so. It looked like a shark. But C.B. said there are a ton of sea turtles out there and I probably saw a turtle or maybe a dolphin."

The Hubs nodded. "Yeah, there are a lot of turtles. They're so cool up close. You should come in the water and see."

I shivered. "No, thank you. This is close enough," I said.

Adolpha tapped my arm. "Mommy, I'm hungry. Can we go get a snack?" she whined. And for the first time in my life I was happy that she was ready to leave some place so I could make her food.

"Absolutely," I said. "Let's get your brother."

ABOUT AN HOUR later we were back at the resort enjoying a snack when the Hubs got a news alert on his phone. He looked up from the screen and announced, "Holy shit, Jen! Shark attack at Hapuna Beach!"

"Hapuna Beach?" Gomer asked around a mouthful of sandwich. "Isn't that where we just were?"

"Yes!" I said, triumphantly. "I told you I saw a shark!"

"Mommy's always right," said Adolpha, licking peanut butter off her fingers.

"I was right! I am vindicated! Take that, C.B.! Sea turtle, my ass!" I pumped a fist in the air and did a spin.

"Damn, Jen, take the celebration down notch," the Hubs said. "Someone could be dead."

"Right," I said, sobering up immediately. "But still, I told C.B.—"

"Where *is* Uncle C.B.?" Gomer asked.

"Surely he's back, right?" the Hubs asked, concerned.

When we left, C.B. and his kids had stayed behind to catch a few more waves. I had no idea if they'd returned to the resort yet or not. "Someone call C.B. Find out where he is. Make sure they're okay," I said.

The Hubs nodded. "Yeah, I'm sure they're fine. They were going to leave right after us. I bet they're not even there anymore."

Now Gomer had pulled up the news story on his phone. "Wait. Dad. There's an update. It says 'Man from *Kansas* Attacked at Hapuna Beach.'"

"What?" I yelled, pulling out my phone. I scanned several articles and saw that the victim was only identified as a man from Kansas who had been surfing with his children. Holy shit. "I told him to get out of there! If he's dead I'm going to be so mad at him. He thinks he's so much smarter than everyone!"

"Mom!" Gomer gasped. "Our local news has the story on Twitter already. They say he's from our town."

"Oh my god. It *is* my brother," I said. "It has to be. What are the odds that there was another man from our town in Kansas at the same beach in Hawaii with his kids? C.B.! You should have listened to me! You should have believed me!"

"Hang on, another update on Twitter," the Hubs said. "Kansas man is alive! He's going to make it."

We all cried out in relief.

I was just fumbling to dial my brother's number when my phone rang. It was C.B. "Hello?" I said.

"You guys didn't go back to the beach, right?" he asked, a little nervous.

"No! Where are you?" I demanded.

"We're at the resort. You saw the news, huh?" C.B. asked.

"Yes! So, you're not the local Kansas man who got bitten by the shark?"

He chuckled. "Yeah, no. And if I did, you wouldn't be my first call."

"True. What the fuck, though?"

"I know, right? We left soon after you guys. We didn't see anything. It must have happened right after we left. I saw an article that said he's a doctor and he told the life-guards how to treat his bite. He basically saved his own life."

Now that I knew my brother and his family were safe and I knew the man from my town was going to live, I felt a wave of relief wash over me. And then came the rage, and I yelled. "I told you I saw a motherfucking shark! Of course I know what a turtle looks like, you dumbass, and it doesn't look like a goddamn shark! You need to believe me next time I tell you to get your ass out of the water. My son could have been a fucking shark meal because I listened to you. Fucking turtle flippers, my ass."

That night before bed I was on my phone researching

how to sell the time share. It was the first time I ever regretted buying the timeshare.

"What are you doing, Jen?" the Hubs asked.

"I'm going to sell our timeshare," I announced. "Our kid could have been attacked by a shark today. The fucking St. Louis Arch never tried to kill us!"

The Hubs nodded. "True. But I really like our vacations, don't you?"

I stopped scrolling and thought about his question. "Yes," I said, sadly. "I'll miss this place."

The Hubs climbed into bed next to me and showed me his phone. "Right? So work smarter! Instead of researching how to sell the timeshare, I've been researching how to treat shark bites."

"Damn. That is dark," I said.

The Hubs shrugged. "I know. I can't help it. This place is magical."

I perked up. "Oooh, speaking of magical," I said. "I've already booked next year's trip."

"We're coming back to Hawaii?" the Hubs asked, his face lighting up.

"Better!" I assured him. "We're going to Disney. They only have alligators that will try and kill you."

TWELVE

THAT TIME I THOUGHT WE WERE GOING TO BE MURDERED IN OUR BEDS. BUT DON'T WORRY, OBVIOUSLY WE WEREN'T SINCE I'M WRITING THIS.

SEATTLE, WASHINGTON

2018

I spend a lot of time on the road promoting my books and speaking to groups. Since I'm away from home a lot, I try to bring the whole family with me whenever I can. A few years ago I was invited to speak in Seattle. Since none of us had ever been, I scheduled the event over spring break so I could bring the Hubs and my kids.

Normally when I travel I get a hotel room and enjoy the king-size bed and TV remote all to myself. Sharing a hotel room with the Hubs and two giant tweens didn't sound like a lot of fun, so I wanted to get a suite, but the hotel rooms were very expensive. So the Hubs suggested we try something new. "Let's rent a house this time."

I wrinkled my nose. "You mean like one of those online sites or whatever?"

"Yeah! We can get a whole house for just a little more than the price of a hotel room. Everyone would have their own room and we'd have a living room to hang out and a kitchen so we could save money eating in."

"I dunno," I said, skeptically. "I'm an old woman and slow to change. I don't like these new-fangled apps the kids are always using. If I refuse to hop in the backseat of some stranger's Civic when there's a perfectly good taxi, bus, or subway close by, I definitely don't want to bunk in some rando dude's house!"

He pulled out his phone and showed me a listing for a cute bungalow. "This one looks nice. And look, a woman owns it. It says here her name's Jessica."

"How do we know it's clean?" I asked. "What if we get bedbugs or something?"

The Hubs scoffed. "I bet it's just as clean as the two-star hotels you stay in. You never question them."

"Yeah, but there's someone to complain to and those are trusted brands. I don't know anything about Jessica's adorable bungalow, or whatever."

"Jen, there are a bunch of reviews. If someone got bedbugs, it would be in the reviews. How about this? I won't pick one that mentions bedbugs, okay?"

"What if the house catches fire in the middle of the night?"

The Hubs looked shocked and then amused. "Wow. Is that how your brain works? Do you really worry about this shit?"

I shrugged. "Sometimes. A hotel room has a map showing me the way to safety. And a hotel has sprinklers."

The Hubs rolled his eyes. "Okay, fine, yes, a hotel has a sprinklers and a house probably doesn't. I can't argue with that. But come on, Jen, you saw how expensive the hotels were. We could only afford one room for all of us. Do you really want to share a hotel room with Gomer and Adolpha? Can you imagine listening to Adolpha's music and smelling Gomer's feet for a week? This way everyone can have their own space, the kids can have some privacy." He wiggled his eyebrows. "*We* can have some privacy."

I was scandalized. "You want to have sex in Jessica's bed?" I hissed.

He laughed. "I want to have sex anywhere I can."

I looked at the picture again. Jessica's house *was* pretty, and I couldn't complain about the cleanliness or her hundreds of five-star reviews. I sighed. "Fine! But you're doing all the cooking. I don't go on vacation to cook!"

And that's how we ended up lost in a neighborhood near downtown Seattle.

The weather in Seattle was bad, so our flight had been delayed and we arrived quite late. Once we wrangled all our luggage into the rental car and got the kids fed (because the sandwiches and snacks I'd packed for the plane didn't count as dinner), we found ourselves driving slowly up and down pitch-black streets trying to find our home away from home.

"What's the number again?" I asked.

"815," the Hubs said, squinting into the darkness. "What does that one say? Is it 900?"

There was a steady rain falling, so I rolled down the window hoping that would give me better vision. "Maybe? Doesn't matter. I can definitely see it ends in a zero, so that's not our house."

"That's 820," Gomer said peering at the house.

"820? So then we must have passed 815, right?" I said, looking into the wet murkiness behind us.

"Who knows?" the Hubs complained. "That one over there is 2000. How do these numbers work?"

"Can you text Jessica and ask her what color the front door is?" I asked, looking closely at the map on my phone. "The GPS says it's definitely right here, but I don't see any bungalows. These are all ranches. Did she bait and switch us?"

"Uh, actually, it's not Jessica's house we're looking for," the Hubs said, glancing at me.

"Excuse me?" I said. I always say excuse me when I'm irritated and need a minute to breathe instead of explode.

"Yeah, well, we took so long discussing it that when we finally made a decisions Jessica's house was no longer available. So I booked Craig's house, instead," the Hubs said.

"Who's Craig?" I asked. "I don't know anything about this Craig person."

"You didn't know anything about Jessica, either. It's still a nice house. It's going to be fine. We just need to find it."

I quickly searched the site for Craig's house.

"I don't care whose house it is. I just wish he'd left a light on," Adolpha grumbled.

"I know, right?" I said. "If we were ever renting out our house, I'd have all the lights on! I'd have pointer signs even! This is ridiculous." At that point we'd been circling the same block for an hour and I was getting tired and angry. I was ready to call the fucking Hilton.

The Hubs pulled over and sent off a text. He got an immediate reply. "Craig says it's a blue house behind a giant hedge. You can't see the house or the number from the street because of the bushes."

"What the f—" I muttered. "Put out a damn pointer sign, then, Craig."

The Hubs kept reading. "He says he can see our car. We're one house away."

"Wait. How can he see our car, Dad?" Gomer asked, looking around nervously. "Where is he?"

"I thought we were renting an empty house," Adolpha said.

"Is he meeting us with the key or something?" I asked.

"All good questions." The Hub consulted his phone.

"Oh, wow, it says here that he lives in the basement of the house."

"What?!" I exclaimed. "Are you kidding me right now? Did you know that when you made the reservation?"

"No, I didn't see that part. I had no idea," the Hubs said. "I guess I missed that."

"You missed it?" I practically yelled. The Hubs has a history of not reading carefully and missing major things. It's one of my biggest pet peeves. I was certain he'd done it again this time.

His phone dinged and he summarized the illuminated message, "He lives in the basement with three roommates and two deadly dogs. He says only go in the front door. Never go in the backyard because the dogs hang out there a lot and will attack."

"Jesus Christ! Where have you taken us?" I demanded.

"Look! There's a giant hedge," Adolpha exclaimed, pointing. "And I think there's a house back there."

We slowly pulled into the dark driveway and all I could think was, *I hope Washington doesn't have a stand-your-ground law because we're going to get shot.*

We rolled up to what appeared to be an abandoned ranch home. Every window was dark and cold. The front yard grew wildly and weeds poked through the gravel driveway. I still couldn't see a visible house number but I did see signs warning of killer dogs on the ten-foot high wooden fence circling the house.

"This has got to be it," the Hubs said, throwing the SUV into park.

"How do you get the key?" I asked. "Will he come out and apologize for not even turning on the porch light for us?"

"I don't think so," the Hubs said. "He's got a lock box on the door and I have the code."

"This is bullshit," I grumbled.

"It's probably just as well, Jen," the Hubs said. "You're in a bad mood and we don't want to make a bad impression. He'll give us a bad rating."

"Right," I said. I didn't give a shit about my rating.

The kids and I stayed in the car and watched the Hubs try the lock box on the front door. It opened easily and he went inside the house. We could see room after room light up as he went through the house.

"Are we really staying here tonight?" Adolpha asked.

"Yes, what choice do we have?" I said, hopping out of the SUV. "Come on, help me get the bags. It's late. You kids should be in bed."

We hauled the suitcases to the door where the Hubs met us, blocking our entry. "Okay, so, it's a bit different than the pictures."

I narrowed my eyes. "How so?" The pictures I'd found moments before showed a light-filled mid-century ranch. The listing boasted a home that was recently remodeled with a new sleek kitchen and shining hardwood floors throughout. The furniture was bright with clean, modern lines.

"You know how it is," the Hubs said. "No house shows well at night."

That was true. Back in my real estate days I rarely showed a house at night. Houses at night typically feel shadowy, cold, and a bit worn.

"Let us in," I said.

The Hubs stepped back and revealed what I can only describe as "Shabby IKEA."

The sleek kitchen was white, but upon closer inspection

we could see where the enamel coating on the cupboards was peeling and yellowing at the corners. The light wood floors were badly scratched from luggage being dragged or rolled across them. The sofas and chairs all had permanent butt indentations that you sunk into as soon as you sat down.

There was a staircase next to the front door that led down to a lower level. "Where does that go?" Gomer asked.

"The basement," the Hubs said. "The owner says it's off-limits. That's where he lives."

"With his three roommates and two killer dogs," I said, eyeing the flimsy plywood door at the bottom of the stairs. I could hear dogs whining and scratching on the other side.

"Let's unpack," the Hubs said.

Once we were in the master bedroom the Hubs said, "I tried the door to the basement."

"And?"

"It's locked. From their side. But there's no way to lock it from our side."

"Well, presumably the owner has a key to every door in the house. He could come inside from any port of entry, correct?"

"Yes," the Hubs looked concerned.

"What about the dogs?" I asked.

"What about them?"

"I'm a bit worried. They're pretty anxious to have us in the house and that door doesn't look sturdy. If they're as dangerous as he says they are, couldn't they break through and eat the kids?"

The Hubs sighed. "Maybe. But the good news is, this house is all on one floor, so if a fire breaks out, there's a window to jump out of in every room."

"Oh, yay!" I said with mock enthusiasm.

Whenever I'm worried and I don't want my kids to know I'm worried, I always pretend like I want them to do something because it would be "so much fun" instead of "Mom's afraid you're going to die!" I didn't like the idea of a strange man (and three roommates and two vicious dogs) living downstairs with access to the house we were sleeping in. Originally we picked a three-bedroom house thinking the kids would each have their own room, but now I didn't want either kid to be alone. One room had bunkbeds, so I suggested it would be "so much fun" to bunk in together. "You guys can stay up late and watch movies on your laptops and talk!" I said, trying way too hard to sell it.

"Actually," Gomer said. "We already talked about it and neither one of us wants to be alone. We were already going to sleep in there together."

I nodded sadly, because poor Gomer. He'd definitely inherited my gift of irrational anxiety.

After we finally unpacked, showered, ate one more snack, and brushed teeth, I got everyone settled into bed.

The Hubs and I left the door to our bedroom open and a light on in the hallway. We tossed and turned for a while and then finally drifted off.

WE HADN'T BEEN asleep for more than an hour when we both sat bolt upright in bed.

"What the fuck was that?" I hissed.

"You heard it too?" the Hubs whispered.

"Yes. It was a door opening, right?"

"I think it was the door to the basement," the Hubs whispered.

We sat quietly, listening intently to the silent house. Then we heard soft footsteps coming up the stairs from the basement. The person stopped at the top of the stairs and waited quietly.

"Are you fucking kidding me right now?" I flew out of bed and assumed my Mama Bear stance: legs apart for maximum stability, hands up for throat-punching and/or eye-gouging, teeth bared for fear factor and biting.

"Shhh!" The Hubs cocked his head and continued listening. "Listen. Someone's opening the front door."

"Are they letting in multiple killers now?" I asked. I pulled on shoes and moved closer to my children sleeping across the hall. I needed shoes because I couldn't curb stomp an intruder in my bare feet!

"Shhh!"

"They know we're here, dummy! Are we just going to sit here and wait to be murdered?"

"Shhh!" The Hubs said again, closing his eyes to think. The Hubs is not a coward, but he's also not a guy who does anything without a plan.

"What's the address?" I demanded, grabbing my cell phone. I wanted to call the police, but I realized I had no clue where I was. I could just see me screaming, "I don't know where I am! It's a blue house behind an enormous fucking hedge on the darkest road in Seattle! Hurry, please, before the dogs eat us!"

I froze when I heard the front door open and close again. And then I heard footsteps slowly descending into the basement. The door at the bottom of the stairs creaked open and shut and I heard a bolt slide firmly into place.

"What the fuck is going on?" the Hubs said. "Why did they come up here?"

"I want to leave," I said.

"Jen, it's three o'clock in the morning. Where will we go?"

"I don't care. I'll sleep in the car. I can't sleep in this house. Not with someone creeping around."

The Hubs nodded. "I hear you. That was very strange."

"Strange? No, it was fucking psycho. Who does that?"

"Well, it is his house..." The Hubs always tries to look on the bright side.

I do not. "I don't give a shit. I'm renting it! Listen, we own rental properties. We don't just sneak in during the middle of the night. We make appointments. In the daylight. That was insane." I'd been terrified a moment before, but now I was raging. I wanted to stomp down the stairs to the basement and bang on the guy's door and demand an explanation for the intrusion.

"I think things are more casual when you use these house-sharing apps."

"Well, clearly I'm not casual! Let's pack up!"

"The problem is, I've paid in advance," the Hubs said. "If we leave, we'll lose our money."

"What? That's stupid. Let's just call customer service and explain to them that things just got weird as fuck and we want to leave."

"It doesn't work that way, Jen. There is no customer service. Not really."

I didn't want to scream, "I told you so!" because that would be unhelpful but I really wanted to scream, "I told you so!" BECAUSE I FUCKING DID!

THERE WAS no way in hell either of were going back to sleep, so the Hubs and I climbed back into our squeaky bed and stared at the ceiling in silence until the sun rose. At the first sign of light, I started packing up.

"So, you don't care if we lose our money?" the Hubs said.

"Yup. I. Don't. Care," I said, throwing my clothes into a suitcase. "Someone came into this house while our kids were sleeping! We're leaving."

"Nothing happened."

"Yet!" I shrieked.

"It's just a couple nights."

"Look at this place." I flung my arms wide. "It's a dump. The daylight doesn't make it look any better than it did last night. There are wild dogs in the basement. There is someone who came into our private space while we were sleeping. I'm done. Text Craig. Tell him we're checking out."

"But what if he has a reasonable explanation?"

"The only explanation I would accept was the basement was flooding and he was going to drown if he didn't come up here and use the front door. Find a number for customer service. I'm getting the kids up."

While I got the kids up and packed, the Hubs tried to reach customer service. I don't know if you've used one of these house-sharing apps before, but they rely heavily on email and chat-bots. The Hubs started with an email explaining that we wanted out of the rental agreement and a full refund. The auto-response was essentially, "I'm a robot. IDGAF. Tough titties. Did this answer your question?"

He kept trying. Finally he asked me to tweet them so we could get a person to talk to us. It worked. (What can I say? When your Twitter handle is @Throat_Punch, corporations tend to respond to you.) A customer service representative called the Hubs and told him that in situations like this the company advises the renter to have a "friendly conversation" with the landlord. They wanted us to go and knock on his door and say, "Hey, man, it really wasn't cool of you to come into our personal space last night. Next time, warn a fella, would ya?"

The Hubs argued, "I really don't want to have a conversation with him. That's what you're for. I shouldn't have to deal with him at all. *You* should deal with him."

The Hubs went round and round. At one point in the conversation it came up that there was a lock on the basement door, but it wasn't on our side of the door, it was on Craig's side. That's what ultimately got the customer service representative's attention. Apparently, that's a big no-no for landlords. But what finally made the difference was the owner had falsely advertised the house would be ours completely.

"I told you I never saw where it said Craig lived here too!" the Hubs crowed. "I was right!" Luckily the Hubs had a screenshot of the description from when he made the reservation, because once we started filing a complaint, the homeowner must have been notified and he changed the description on the site.

Finally, the company allowed us to cancel our reservation but instead of refunding our money, though, they said we'd have a "credit" to use at another property in the city. "We have to stay in another stranger's house?" I complained.

"Yes. It's the only way to get out of here and not lose our money," the Hubs said. He looked beat. He'd been working for hours to get this far and we both knew it was the best offer he was going to get.

I sighed. "Fine. But I want a house to ourselves."

"Yeah, that's the problem," he said. "I looked and there's not a lot available that we can afford."

"What does that mean?"

"All the houses in our price range are taken. But I did find something interesting," he said.

I narrowed my eyes. "Explain 'interesting.'"

The Hubs quickly explained that he'd found a mansion for rent—or at least part of a mansion. "We don't get the whole mansion. The house is 15,000 square feet and we get our own personal wing. A family lives there. Two parents, two kids, two *friendly* dogs. We share the kitchen and living room with the family and they don't come in our wing at all and we don't go in their wing. We're completely separated inside the house."

"I don't know…"

"It's the only option we have, Jen, unless you want a studio apartment downtown."

I was tired of fighting and I didn't want to spend another night in Craig's house nor did I want to share a studio with my family. "Fine!"

WITHIN AN HOUR we were pulling into a private drive. The asphalt cut a path through a heavily wooded lot. I peered around a corner and there was the house. It was a beautiful home situated on a park-like setting with multiple outdoor patios and a garden. "Wow!" Gomer exclaimed.

"I wonder if they put out signs at night," Adolpha grumbled. "This would be impossible to find."

We followed the driveway around the back of the house to the eight-car garage. All the doors were open and we could see a few pricey cars on display. A man stood in the driveway, motioning us to the spot where he wanted us to park.

"Are we sure this is the right place?" I asked.

"I'll find out." The Hubs hopped out of the SUV and went to speak to the man.

After a few minutes he returned.

"Is this where we're staying, Dad?" Gomer asked.

"Yup. This is it. Okay, here's the deal, though. They weren't expecting guests and they just had new carpet put down today. Shoes off here in the garage and be careful you don't scuff the walls carrying in the luggage. We're going up to the second floor."

Everyone grabbed a bag and we made our way through the house to our wing. A tiny woman was vacuuming my bedroom. She was in a skin-tight dress and barefoot. She turned off the vacuum when she saw me. "Hi! I'm Joan," she said. "I'm sorry I'm in your room. I'm never here, but I wanted to vacuum the new carpet before you got here. I'm done now."

"I understand," I said.

"Leave your things here and come in the kitchen. We'll go over the rules," she said.

I followed her into the massive kitchen. She pointed out a wall dominated entirely by three enormous refrigerators. "This one is ours, do not go in there. That's our food. This one is yours. It's empty. Fill it with groceries if you want. We don't touch your food. This one is all drinks. Bottled water, cans of soda, juice boxes, whatever. That's for everyone. Feel free to help yourself. You can use the kitchen and cook. You clean it when you're done. I cook dinner every night. Usually at eight. I will want the kitchen to myself then."

"We have dinner plans every night we're here," I said. "So we won't be in your way. We'll probably get some cereal for breakfast and then we'll be gone all day."

"You don't get cupboards. Keep your cereal in the fridge."

Okaaaaay.

"These are your plates and glasses." Joan pointed to a motley collection of plastic wear. "Don't use ours."

It might have seemed like Joan had a lot of rules, but I actually liked the clear boundaries. I appreciated that we had ground rules and dos and don'ts.

"My kids will be home from school soon. They will want to play with your kids. You okay with that? Otherwise I'll keep them away."

I shook my head. "No, I'm okay with that. I think my kids would like that."

"Good. I'll show you the common room." Joan flung open a set of double doors to reveal a large game room. A pit sofa was in the middle of the room facing a giant television. A pool table and a poker table anchored one end of the room and a bar anchored the other. The bar had locks on the cabinet doors. "You can drink alcohol, but you have to get your own. And you can't drink after ten o'clock. We learned the hard way people get too loud and rowdy after that."

Gomer immediately grabbed a pool cue and started shooting pool. "Gomer!" I hissed.

"It's okay," Joan said, smiling. "That's what this room is for. You can play in here all night. Well, except for pool. My husband hates when people play pool after midnight. He says he can hear it."

"Oh, that won't be a problem," I said. "We'll be in bed by midnight."

"My husband said you had trouble at your last house?"

I nodded.

"What happened?"

"Not sure, exactly. We were supposed to have the house to ourselves, but the owner was in the basement and he came up into our area in the middle of the night."

Joan looked shocked. "What for?"

"Not sure. He said he needed to throw out our trash. We'd just arrived a few hours before. We didn't have that much trash."

"That's not normal!" Joan said.

"I wouldn't know. That was our first time renting a house."

"Oh no!" Joan exclaimed. "Normally it's a really good experience. We've met some really nice people over the years."

"Well, I think this is going to be fine. Your home is beautiful. We have our own designated space. You have hard and fast rules. And you didn't tell me that your dogs might eat us. So far, so much better!"

"Sometimes people think we're too strict, but this our house. We live here too. We have to have rules, because people do dumb stuff."

I nodded. I liked Joan.

OUR NEXT FEW days at Joan's house were uneventful. We kept our cereal in the fridge and cleaned up after ourselves. We shut down the game room by eleven o'clock every night and we never found Joan or her husband lurking in our rooms in the middle of the night.

I'm not a convert, though. It was still a strange feeling to be in someone's house and know nothing about them. They seemed nice because they had a beautiful home, cute kids, and friendly dogs, but if I was going to be a serial killer, I'd get all those things too to make my victims feel at ease.

I was so obsessed with how I felt about being in a stranger's house, I never really thought about how the owners feel having strangers in their guest rooms. I didn't think about them going to bed at night, worrying about the creeper in the guest wing. It wasn't until the last morning our stay that I thought about this. The Hubs was packing the car and I was feeding the kids breakfast when I remembered the melon I'd bought. "We need to eat that melon this morning," I said.

I looked in my designated cupboard but I couldn't find a cutting board and all my cutlery was plastic. Joan was working in her office off the kitchen. I knocked softly on her door.

"Yes?" Joan called.

"Is there a cutting board we can use?"

Joan opened the door. "A cutting board?" she asked, suspiciously.

I was surprised. "Yes, we have a melon we bought. I'd like to cut it up so the kids can eat it for breakfast. I'd be happy to leave the leftovers for your family."

"We don't take anyone's leftovers. We don't know you," Joan said.

I was a bit hurt. Did she think I'd poison her family or something? What the hell? "It's just, I'd hate to see it go to waste."

"Next time you should buy melon already cut up," Joan advised.

I nodded.

Joan walked toward the kitchen, still talking. "We don't usually give out knives. I'll do it just this once, because you didn't know. And my kids are at school and it's your last day. But normally we don't do knives. Ever." She pulled an enormous ring of keys from a drawer and found the one she was looking for. She climbed up on a chair and reached for a padlocked cupboard at the top of her cabinets. I'd never noticed that cupboard before. It was small and hidden in a corner. She stuck the key in the padlock and opened it. Inside was a butcher block of knives. She pulled out one knife and a cutting board and then locked the cupboard again. She handed the items to me before she climbed down off the chair.

"Why are your knives locked up?" Adolpha asked.

"Because only crazy people would choose to stay in a stranger's house," Joan said, heading back to her office.

THIRTEEN

HEY LADY, THIS SOUNDS LIKE A YOU PROBLEM AND NOT A ME PROBLEM

ATLANTA, GEORGIA

2018

When I announced the publication of *Working with People I Want to Punch in the Throat* on my social media accounts in 2017, a reader asked, "Are you going to go on book tour?"

I groaned when I saw the question. I knew I needed to promote the book, but to be honest, I wasn't very comfortable with the whole book tour thing. I'd done a small tour in 2014 when the first *People I Want to Punch in the Throat* book was released, and it had not gone well. I'd done a terrible job promoting it, so turnout was low, and my speaking skills were shit. I was super intimidated and way too nervous to get up in front of a crowd—even a small one.

But rather than admit the truth and be vulnerable about my shortcomings, I cracked a joke. "No, I'd rather come to Albany and meet you and ten of your friends at the local bar. We'll have some drinks, some laughs, and I'll sell you some books there!"

I thought my off-the-cuff remark would get me a laugh and I'd move on. Instead, my inbox blew up with invitations: "I'll host you in Maryland!" "What do I have to do to get you to Minneapolis?" "Any chance you're going to be in Dallas anytime soon?"

I was surprised by the response, but still didn't quite know what to do with it all. That night I mentioned it to the Hubs. "It would be hilarious if I just showed up in Dallas, or whatever, right?" I laughed.

The Hubs wasn't laughing. He never laughs when he's brewing up seriously great ideas. "You should go to Dallas. And Maryland and Minneapolis."

"Are you kidding?" I asked.

"No. You should go on the road and promote the book."

"But I'm not good at book tours. Remember when I sat by myself in that bookstore in Iowa?" "Yes. You should do a book tour, but you should do it like a Tupperware party!" he said.

"Wait. What?" I was utterly confused. "Have you ever been to a Tupperware party?"

"No, but listen. Tupperware parties have hostesses, right? The Tupperware lady—that's you—signs up hostesses to have a party. The hostess invites her friends to the party and the Tupperware lady sells her plasticware. You could do that."

I was still confused. "I don't sell Tupperware."

The Hubs was getting exasperated. "Jen! You'll sell books. Only you'll pre-sell them. You won't get on a plane until the hostess has at least twenty-five people signed up and paid for."

"I won't make any money that way," I argued. I'm not good at math, but I'm not terrible and twenty-five people would barely cover my airfare.

The Hubs shook his head. "You'll make a profit if you bring other books with you. But it's really about marketing yourself and improving your speaking skills so you'll be better for your next book tour."

So for the next year, I crisscrossed the country attending my version of Tupperware parties, except with books. It started out with meetups in bars and restaurants and people's kitchens and then my readers got even more creative. I was invited to speak at several of their companies, civic organizations, and local libraries. I was even asked to speak at a few churches and schools. (Yes, yes, I know what you're thinking, but believe it or not, I can be G-rated if I have to!)

The Hubs was right. It was a great lesson for me and over time, I honed my skills and figured out how to entertain a crowd—any kind of crowd. I also learned how to think on my feet and tailor my message to a particular group.

At the end of my prepared speech I always asked if there were any questions.

Inevitably someone would ask me what I do about "haters" in the crowd. Sure, I've been called all sorts of names on the internet. I've received hateful emails and even some angry snail mail. I've been left comments that would make you see stars. I've even had people walk out of my public presentations, but I'd never had a problem with any of my in-person events organized by my readers. Because my readers were the ones typically hosting me, the crowds were usually quite friendly. They'd been "warned" about me and my salty tongue and my strong opinions on every-fuckingthing. Many of them had already read a book or two of mine before they even came out to see me. Most of them were "my people."

. . .

AND THEN I was invited to Atlanta by my friend Stephanie.

Whenever a potential hostess contacts me, I let them know I'm really easy to work with and I just need the basics:

- I need her to find and book a venue that can hold everyone.
- I need her to take care of getting twenty-five people into the room.

Anything else a hostess wants to do is gravy.

Stephanie is one of those rare, insanely likable over-achievers. She's an extroverted extrovert. She's a connector of people. She never needs an excuse to throw a party. She loves to plan epic celebrations and she's fucking great at it. When Stephanie heard my requirements, she laughed in my face. She didn't want to book a private room in a dingy bar somewhere in downtown Atlanta. She wanted to find a space worthy of her party-planning talents! To Stephanie, twenty-five people was a small get-together. She wanted to invite over one hundred people!

I told Stephanie to do her thing and just tell me when and where to show up.

Stephanie paired up with Dennis, a colleague of hers who owned a gorgeous venue that had just opened. She pitched the idea that Dennis would provide the space and she'd invite all her friends and business associates to the party. Dennis liked the idea so much he asked if he could also invite people to the event. Since Stephanie's loves meeting new people she readily agreed.

The night of the event arrived and Stephanie did not disappoint. She'd clearly called every contact in her phone and convinced them to come, so the place was packed. Stephanie worked the room like a pro and introduced me to everyone. I quickly figured out it was an eclectic mix of her friends and neighbors, former and potential clients, and business associates. Dennis had not invited as many people as Stephanie, but he also had a good showing.

When it was time to start the "show" we gathered in the ballroom and I got going. By then I was a seasoned speaker and entertainer. I started my prepared speech, but I always play to the audience and let them sort of dictate where we go. That night the group's energy was off the charts, and I could feel my energy ramp up too. It was such a fabulous group, so I just kept going longer and I told a few more stories than usual, trying to get bigger laughs. They were laughing their asses off having a fan-fucking-tastic time and so was I. One woman even snorted, which is truly the highest praise you could give me. I try not to overthink when I'm speaking or I'll forget where I'm going, but I distinctly remember thinking that night, *"Holy shit, this group is amazing. I could do this all night!"*

But all good things must come to an end, so I finally wound down and like always, I asked if anyone had any questions.

A woman in the back raised her hand. Once she stood up, I recognized her. We were never formally introduced but I remembered her clearly from earlier in the night. She'd arrived with a crew of Dennis' friends and purchased a $20 book with a $100 bill. When I tried to make change for her, she told me to keep it as a tip.

"That's a nice tip, Hilda!" her friend had exclaimed.

She waved a hand and said, "Oh, it's fine!"

In all my various careers, no one has ever tipped me, so I

remembered Hilda and her generosity. When Hilda stood, I could see she was crying. I was a little surprised—kind of. Here's the thing; I get criers at my events, that part wasn't unusual. A lot of people are in dark places when they discover my work and they pick it up and find some momentary relief from the pain they're experiencing. They get to laugh for a bit and forget their worries. However, they always find me after the event and cry privately. They usually take me into a corner and we cry together, because for me, the hardest part about the criers is keeping myself from crying too. To see Hilda crying in front of everyone was a bit jarring and all I could think was, *Keep it together, Jen. Stay strong, no matter what. Her child died of cancer. Her husband left her. Whatever it is, be sympathetic and kind, but don't make it weird and fucking bawl.*

I smiled warmly at Hilda and nudged her to ask her question. "Hi, what's your question?"

But Hilda didn't ask a question, instead she started in immediately on a rambling, incoherent word salad. It was so shocking that I can't even remember exactly what she said, but it boiled down to something like this:

"I just have to interrupt you because I need to say something," she sobbed.

"Okay, go ahead," I encouraged. *Smile, Jen. Do. Not. Cry.*

"Tonight...has been..." She gulped.

Amazing...wonderful...spectacular...   I   thought, motioning for her to continue.

"So..." Her body trembled.

Oh, let it out, sister. We're all here for you.

She hiccupped. "Negative."

THE FUCK DID SHE JUST SAY???

A woman in the front row whipped around in her seat and yelled, "Have you even been listening?"

Hilda ignored her and kept going, "This has been nothing but a night of absolute man-bashing. You have attacked men and I feel like I need to speak up for them! Someone has to!" She sobbed hysterically. "I am a good Christian woman who has raised two good Christian sons. I am married to a good man who works hard and makes good money. They are good men! And my son!—" Hilda hiccupped again, loudly. "My son, who is so good—*so good* —can't get into college because women are taking his place!"

My brain was racing. *I'm sorry, but what the fuck is happening right now, Jen?* I thought. I was taken aback by her fucking bizarre and nonsensical speech. Everyone was. Except for the woman who yelled at her, everyone else was quiet. The room was absolutely silent.

Hilda exclaimed, "I just feel like you're just pushing down men and downgrading men and we need to raise our boys to be good Christian men. *This*," she gestured wildly around the room, "is not good for men! It's not good to bash our men!"

Stephanie was in the front row and I could see her turning around and straining to see Hilda. We made eye contact and she sort of shrugged like, "I have no clue what's going on." This was not what I expected at all. I was unsure what to do. So, I just kept listening. And Hilda kept talking.

She continued, "And you're doing nothing to help. I'm raising good Christian sons who will be good to your daughters!"

By that time I could see that Hilda was not doing well. She was incapacitated and incoherent. I was getting irritated, but I was trying to keep my cool because I didn't want to embarrass

Stephanie in front of her guests. But I also wanted to correct Hilda. She was mad at me for bashing men and assumed I only had daughters even though I'd spoken about both my kids, but she wasn't fucking listening. I interjected and said, "Thank you. I'm raising a good son too along with my daughter. But I think you misunderstood what I was saying. I'm saying I'm trying to teach my son to leave space for my daughter and other girls. I don't want to lower the bar for him, I'm just trying to boost my daughter so she can actually reach it."

She flipped out. "And I'm saying that this night was so negative and I can't believe it!"

The two women seated on either side of Hilda tried to console her and get her to sit down. She shoved them away. "I'm *fiiiinnnne*," she slurred. One of the women looked at me and mimed drinking out of a cup—the international symbol for "she's drunk as fuck."

Oh, great, I thought bitterly. Normally I like events with an open bar because people who imbibe a bit laugh louder and buy more books, but tonight, all that free wine was backfiring on me.

As her friends wrestled her back into her chair, Hilda took one last swipe at me. "It's not his fault that my husband is more successful than the women he works with," she bellowed.

That's when my temper started to flare. Up until that point, I'd been pretty cool listening to Hilda berate me, but now I'd had enough. She was obviously fucked up and she wanted to air her grievances with me and I was fine with letting her air them, but when she said that, something clicked inside of me.

I could feel so many responses perking up in my reptilian brain. You see, when I get that sort of comment online, I unload with a list of expletives and links to stats showing everything from women's pay inequality to the attack on women's reproductive rights. I let them know about our lack of representation everywhere power is held. I usually close with an invitation for them to go fuck themselves along with the ban stick. But I couldn't do that there.

So I took a deep breath to slow my brain and heart rate. Because here's the thing, this was not some keyboard warrior trolling my social media pages from her mom's basement. This wasn't even a stranger who had wandered in off the street to hear me speak in a public forum. Everyone in that room was somehow connected to Stephanie or Dennis. I knew Hilda probably wasn't Stephanie's client or colleague, but I couldn't be certain. If nothing else, she was connected to Hilda through Dennis and I knew Dennis was an important business contact for Stephanie. If I went scorched earth on Hilda, I would include Stephanie (and possibly her business and reputation) in that blast. I could decimate Hilda right there and leave nothing but a pile of ash, because I would never have to see her again, but Stephanie probably did. Maybe their kids went to school together? Maybe she and Stephanie worked out at the same gym? Maybe Hilda was a potential client Stephanie had been trying to land? I couldn't risk it.

I had just made a deal with myself to try and be a kinder, gentler Jen who doesn't just destroy everything around her and I felt like the Universe was testing me. I also didn't want to make anything uncomfortable for Stephanie and her guests. Stephanie had worked tirelessly to organize such an incredible night and 99.9% of the attendees were amazing. The fuck I was going to let Hilda ruin anything for anyone!

The room was thick with tension. Everyone's head was on a swivel between me and Hilda—waiting to see what I'd say. They all know the title of my books. They all heard my disclaimer at the beginning of the night when I said, "I'm going to say a lot of snarky things and if you don't have a sense of humor, you should probably leave now." Hilda should have walked out the door at that point instead of to the fucking bar. I would have happily returned her $100 bill.

I looked at Stephanie. She looked irritated, but I couldn't tell if she was irritated with me or Hilda. Dennis was hiding in the kitchen.

I had to squash Hilda and her nonsense. She'd had her time, but no one had come out that night to hear her bull-shit. They came to hear me. So, instead of taking Hilda's bait, I changed the subject and moved on, ignoring Hilda's continued sobbing. I took away her light and her oxygen, because that's what you do when you're being attacked by someone. They can only hurt you if you let them. They can only feel emboldened when they're given attention, so I decided to let Hilda and her idiocy die in the dark.

Hilda stayed in her seat and continued to cry and bemoan her experience but she didn't speak directly to me again. I took a few more questions, but the night was kind of soured at that point. The high-octane energy from earlier was gone and people were feeling awkward after Hilda's outburst.

Finally, Stephanie saved the day. "Hey Jen," she said. "Could you tell one more story, please?"

"Um, sure," I said, flipping through my mental Rolodex of stories I can tell off the top of my head.

"I have one I'd like my friends to hear," Stephanie said.

"Oh, perfect! Which one?"

"The one you told us last night at dinner," Stephanie said, smiling broadly.

The night before I'd gone to dinner with Stephanie and a couple of her close friends. The only story I'd told was about a rumor I'd heard about the moms at a local Christian school. It was a status symbol for the moms at this school to carry a particular handbag. And when I went on my blog and publicly wondered about the women's fascination with this bag, I was told it's privately called the "in-the-butt-bag" because your husband only buys you one when you let him perform a certain—*ahem*—act with you. Even though I use the f-bomb like a comma, the butt bag story is not one I ever tell in public. It is a raunchy story that could easily offend half the room (especially if they were like Hilda).

I looked at Stephanie and she looked at me. "Really?" I asked. "You want *that* story?"

Stephanie smiled coolly and I could see she was ready to blow shit up. She did not give a fuck anymore. She threw a glance back toward Hilda. "Absolutely," she said. "And don't leave out any of the details."

Since I am not one to back down from telling a hilarious story (and I'd already pissed off Hilda), I took another deep breath and said, "Okay, so there's this local Christian school where a select group of moms carry a particular hand-bag..."

The in-the-butt-bag story killed. People were falling off their chairs laughing so hard. As I said, it's not my usual fare, but for that group and for that night, that story was exactly what we needed to get back on track.

As for Hilda? I really don't know she reacted to the story. I learned a long time ago that if someone isn't feeling me, my job isn't to convince them. She'd already wasted so much of my energy that night and was such a fucking drag that I didn't even look at her while I told the story. I do know she stayed at the party all night because any time I came within earshot of her, she'd let out a huge, fake laugh and turn her back on me. Typical mean girl bullshit but weirder since she was 60 years old.

I will always remember that night as my first experience with a heckler. When I called the Hubs after and told him about Hilda, he simply said, "Congratulations. Now you've arrived. Hopefully, Denver likes you better tomorrow night."

FOURTEEN

DID I EVER TELL YOU I FOUGHT A RACCOON IN AN AIRPORT PARKING LOT?

KANSAS CITY, MISSOURI

2018

I'd been on the road for two weeks when I landed at the Kansas City International Airport at midnight. The airport is already a sleepy little place, but at midnight it was especially quiet. My flight had been full, but almost everyone just had a carry-on, so the terminal emptied out quickly. There were only about twenty of us waiting at the baggage carousel and I swear my bags were the last ones to drop down the slide to the belt below.

As I struggled to get them off the carousel, I saw the bus to the parking lot pull up outside. "Shit," I said, throwing my back into my work and tugging even harder on the suitcase handle. The buses to the satellite parking were notoriously few and far between during the peak hours, but at midnight, it could be an hour before another one came along—if another one came along. "I'm coming," I yelled to the empty building as I yanked my last bag off the belt.

Luckily, it was the end of my trip and not the beginning. I'd sold a suitcase of books, so half my luggage was empty. Empty or not, they were still a pain in the ass to maneuver. I ran awkwardly, pulling and pushing my bags. "Wait for me!" I yelled again as I burst through the doors of the airport.

The bus driver heard me and thankfully waited while I wrangled my bags up the stairs of the bus. No one moved to help me. It was fine. I was used to it. I get it. I'm a strong, capable woman who packed a lot of fucking shit, so I needed to deal with it. But at midnight, I wouldn't say no to a little help hoisting a fifty-pound suitcase up the bus steps. Especially since I'm only five feet nothing and the steps hit me above my knees. It's a fucking leap for me to get up there. I got myself and my baggage onto the bus and thanked everyone for waiting for me. Everyone stared at me, bleary-eyed.

As the bus drew closer to the parking lot I started to panic. "Where did I park?" I muttered. I checked my phone. A lot of times I take a picture of the row number or I text the Hubs the information, but this time it appeared I'd forgotten. "Damn it." I wracked my brain.

I had caught a 6:00 a.m. flight out, so it was dark when I parked my car. Plus I had been running late. I had to make a run for the bus that morning (with fully loaded bags) and I must have been too distracted (and out of breath) to make a note of my van's parking coordinates.

No worries, I thought. The bus stops at about fifteen covered shelters. It can take a while, so normally I try to park among the first spots that get dropped off. I often land after midnight and I just want to get the fuck out as quickly as possible. As we pulled up to Bus Stop One, I looked around for my silver Honda minivan. Do you know how many people in Kansas City drive silver Honda minivans? A fuck ton. Ugh.

Even with all the vans to choose from, I didn't see mine. I've got a Ruth Bader Ginsburg air freshener hanging from the rearview mirror and she kind of stands out. I didn't see RBG anywhere. I wasn't surprised. It's always a lucky day if you can find an open spot near the first stop. I would have remembered a fluke like that.

Must be Bus Stop Two, I thought.

The bus trudged to the next shelter and when it came to a stop next to a matte black Mercedes G-Wagon, I was positive that was my stop. I distinctly remembered admiring a matte black Mercedes G-Wagon while I waited for the bus the morning I left. I threw my suitcases out the bus door and jumped out after them. The bus driver practically shut the doors on my ass. He was ready to get the fuck out, too.

Suddenly, I was all alone in the dark and empty parking lot. Normally, I'm not afraid to be out on my own after dark, but that night I got a little chill thinking of all the what-ifs. I was in a remote location and I still wasn't sure where my car was. I looked around, but I couldn't see Ruth's welcoming lace collar beckoning me home.

Whenever I can't find my car (which is more often than I care to admit), I'm that asshole who sets off her car alarm so she can follow the racket. I figured I was all alone and wouldn't offend anyone, so I dug out my keys and started clicking the button on my fob.

Nothing happened.

"Shit," I grumbled, hitting the button repeatedly. The wind blew. It was a blustery, chilly fall night. I'd been traveling down south and didn't bring a coat, mostly to save space in my four suitcases. While packing I decided that shoes I'd wear several times were more important than a coat I'd wear once. I shivered and looked at my cute, impractical, sandals.

I continued to spin around in a circle, hitting the fob. That's when I saw way down by Bus Stop Three another matte black G-wagon. "Motherfucker," I complained. "I got off too soon."

I jammed my keys into my pocket and grabbed my shit and started the slow progress to Bus Stop Three.

Now, it's usually at this point that a smart person asks me why I didn't just leave all my luggage, go find the van, and *then* come back for it all. I have no good answer for that question other than with my luck I'd probably forget where I left my luggage and then I'd be doubly fucked. At least if I had my suitcases, I felt like I could survive the night if needed.

When I got down to the Bus Stop Three, I started hitting the alarm button again. Now I was doubly certain I was in the right spot. I was sure I remembered arriving in the lot to find Bus Stop Two full, so I had to go all the way to Three. My van was definitely in this area. I swung my arm around trying to trigger my car, but it was still silent.

I decided to try something I'd read about on the internet.

I don't know how key fobs work, exactly. I mean, I'm not an engineer. Or a science person. I'm a writer, for fuck's sake. But I'd read on a random site somewhere that if you're in a parking lot and need to "boost the signal" on your key fob, you should put it on your head so your body will "act like an antenna" and increase the range. I have no idea if this is true or not. I'm not trying to teach you shit about how things work, so if I'm wrong, please don't send me hate mail, okay? But if I'm right, then you're welcome!

It had been an hour since I'd landed and I was standing in the middle of a dark and desolate parking lot with a keyless remote on my head trying to be a motherfucking antenna when my cellphone rang.

It was the Hubs. "Where are you?" he asked.

"I'm still in the parking lot," I sobbed. "I can't find my car!"

"What do you mean? You can't remember where you parked?"

"No! I didn't text the information to you. Why didn't you remind me?" I screeched. When I'm frustrated, I tend to take it out on the Hubs. I understand logically it's not his fault that I forgot where I parked my car. But at nearly one o'clock in the morning, I was in no mood for logic.

"So, how are you going to find it?" he asked. "I don't know!" I wailed.

"Well, what have you tried? Besides standing there crying?" he asked. Always the fixer!

"I've got the key on my head! The head thing doesn't work!"

"What?"

"The key! It's on my head. I'm being an antenna or whatever."

"Oh! Yeah, that actually works," he said. "It's actually pretty cool. It's because of your oral cavity and the fluids in your head. They—"

"Oh my god, shut the fuck up! I need to find my car. I'm so tired. I'm cold. I'm a little scared, even."

The Hubs scoffed. "You're not scared of anything."

"Well, I'm scared of dying in this godforsaken place. It's like a ghost town out here. Everyone is gone. The wind blows and I think it's someone behind me. In fact, I feel like someone's watching me right now."

"No one's watching you, Jen," the Hubs said. "The parking lot is secure. There's no one out there, except maybe a security guard. Go to one of the shelters and call the airport. See if they'll send a bus to drive you around to look for your car."

For once he had a good idea. "Okay, I'll call you later."

I dragged my stuff to the nearest bus stop shelter and picked up the emergency phone. "Hello?" a man said.

"Hello. I'm at Bus Stop Four and I can't find my car. Is there another bus out here than can help me? Or maybe security?"

"Buses are pretty much done for the night," the man said. "And security patrols every hour, or so. Keep an eye out for a white pick-up truck." And then he hung up on me before I could say anything else.

Here's the weird thing about me, a lot of times people assume I'm a "Karen." They think I'm the middle-aged woman who will flip a fucking table if she can't use her expired $.25 off coupon at the grocery store. But I'm really not. I try not to be trouble or a pain, so when he hung up on me, I was pissed, but I was more pissed at myself. *I'd* caused this problem. *I* was the one who hadn't paid attention to where *I'd* parked *my* car. *I* was the who was too cheap to use the airport valet. *I* was the one who wanted to travel around the fucking country to promote my book. *I* was the one who enjoyed meeting my readers. And *I* was definitely the one who loved having a hotel room all to myself for the past two weeks!

Arggh!! I was still trying to figure out what to do when I heard a noise behind me. I hadn't seen another person for at least an hour or so. *It's just the wind again,* I thought. *There is no one out here with me.* I continued to mash the button on my key to no avail. I heard the noise again. This time it was closer.

I whipped around, expecting to see nothing and have a good laugh at my nervousness, but instead I was confronted by an enormous raccoon. It was about ten feet away from me. He was baring his teeth and his beady eyes gleamed in the dim light.

"Fuck!" I screamed.

My scream startled the raccoon. Instead of fleeing, it raised up on his hind legs and growled at me. He spread his arms wide and stretched his body to his full three-foot height.

As I stood there trying to understand what was happening, several things rushed through my mind:

- *I didn't even know raccoons could stand on their hind legs.*
- *That's kind of terrifying.*
- *Oh shit, that thing wants to fight.*
- *Does that little fucker look normal pissed off or rabid pissed off?*

And finally:

- *Not today, motherfucker. I'm in no mood for your shit.*

I threw my bags to the ground and assumed my fighting position (which ironically, was very similar to the raccoon's fighting position). We faced off, teeth bared, claws out, ready to battle.

Now, I realize that the title of this book might make you think I know how to fight, but I do not. My weapon of choice is the keyboard. Unless I was going to kill the raccoon with sarcasm and excellent grammar, this was going to be a quick fight. And I was going to lose.

Can you imagine the humiliation my family would suffer when they had to announce to my readers that I'd been killed by a rabid raccoon in the economy lot of the Kansas City airport? (Actually, my readers would probably be like, "Yeah, that seems legit.")

I needed a plan! But I had no idea what my plan was except "survive." But I couldn't see a way out. I'm slow as fuck. You want me on your zombie apocalypse team because I'll be eaten first and you can run while the zombies are enjoying the all-you-can-eat buffet that is Jen.

And then I remembered an article I'd read about a young woman who was attacked by a rabid raccoon while she was on a walk in the woods. She killed it with her bare hands. It attacked her and she was so desperate to save herself she had to improvise. She strangled the animal and then drowned it in a puddle near the trail. I looked around but the parking lot was dry. Not a murderous puddle in sight.

Fine.

I was going to have to improvise another way. I picked up my crossbody bag and started swinging it by the strap in giant circles. I figured I might make contact with the ring-tailed bastard and launch it across the parking lot like Babe Ruth.

If anyone was watching me they would have thought I'd lost my mind. Here was a woman surrounded by discarded luggage, howling in the night and swinging a purse over her head.

The raccoon didn't move. He just stood there watching me closely, his little raccoon fingers opening and closing. Oh shit! He was imagining strangling me and drowning me in puddle. He'd read the same article! I had to act quickly, but I knew he was too fast for me. My only chance was to make the first move and catch him by surprise.

I took a deep breath and screamed, "Come at me, bro!" I

lunged at the raccoon and threw my purse toward it. Immediately, the expression on its face changed. It was no longer menacing and, if I'm not mistaken, I'm pretty sure I saw a flash of fear cross its eyes. If a raccoon could say, "Fuck this shit, that lady's crazy," it would have. The raccoon dropped to all fours and scurried off into the darkness between two parked cars.

I practically collapsed with relief because that was the one and only move I had. I wasn't prepared for mortal combat with a giant rodent!

I breathed a huge sigh of relief and collected the luggage strewn around me. I shot a nervous look over to where the raccoon had disappeared, hoping he wasn't planning his retaliation. The raccoon was gone...for now. But I still needed to find my van. It was dark, but something familiar caught my eye. I took a closer look at the cars the raccoon had run between and saw that one car was a Ford sedan and the second car was a Honda minivan with a motherfucking Ruth Bader Ginsberg air freshener hanging from the rearview mirror.

I didn't believe in angels before that day but I do now! You can try and tell me angels are big and bright with fluffy wings and harps, but I won't believe you. I know angels look exactly like trash pandas.

FIFTEEN

BOOKS, BALLS, AND BEDLAM

ST. LOUIS, MISSOURI

2019

I'm kind of a curmudgeon. I typically consider large groups of people a big "fuck no." But I make an exception for book nerd stuff. I love attending writing conferences or book conventions. I'll gladly put on pants to wait in line to get an autograph from a favorite author. I'll even happily wear a bra to teach a class on book publishing. It's even better when these book people events happen close enough to home that I can drive rather than slog through an airport!

So, I was thrilled when I secured a spot at a popular conference in St. Louis. I'd never been to this particular conference before, but I'd followed the event online for years and knew a little about what to expect.

I was excited when the date finally rolled around. I threw everything into my minivan and set off across the great state of Missouri. It's funny, because Missouri is called "The Show-Me State," but there's really nothing to show you except billboards advertising nude dancers, gun shows, and God. I always marvel at the Venn diagram of individuals these messages are targeting. Every time I drive to St. Louis I think someone should just open a church with a choir full of strippers and a gift shop that sells Bibles and guns. I think they'd make a fortune, actually.

My drive was uneventful. I didn't find God, tip a stripper, or buy a gun. I just hit the cruise control, sang my tunes, and ate gummy bears. When I rolled into St. Louis around midday, I pulled up to a hotel that can only be described as "murdery." In fact, I drove by it twice, because I was positive my GPS was drunk when she announced, "You've arrived." All I could see was an abandoned warehouse surrounded by a gaggle of sketchy-looking men. On my third pass, I saw the sign announcing that the dilapidated building I kept ignoring was indeed the hotel I was looking for. *Oh shit. That's not a building scheduled for demolition? That's where I'm sleeping tonight? I've made a terrible mistake.*

When attending conferences I always like to stay at the official conference hotel because it's easier to get to and from late night events or hang out with new friends in the lobby bar. I don't usually do much research on the hotel before I get there, figuring *how bad can it be?*

At this moment I realized the answer to my stupid fucking question.

I went around the corner one last time to make sure I wasn't missing a five-star hotel with the same exact name just one block over. On my final pass, I really took in the neighborhood where I'd be living for the next few days. I figured out that the loitering men were a result of the very busy bus depot and train station across the street. *Purrrrfect.*

I pulled up to the hotel and hopped out of the car to check in. A man from the hotel asked if I want my car valeted.

The Hubs would kill me if I paid for valet, so I said,

"No thank you, I'm just checking in and then I'm leaving again. I have to go to a meeting downtown."

"Okay, but make sure you lock your car, ma'am."

"Here? In the driveway?" I asked.

"Yes ma'am. It's best not to leave it too long, either." His casual yet insistent warnings became the mantra of the weekend.

Every time I met an attendee who was from out of town they'd ask me, "Do you think it's safe here? My Uber driver didn't even want to drop me off."

"I told a waitress where I was staying and she said I need to be careful."

"I heard there was a murder at this hotel recently."

Look, I lived in New York City for years. I have street-smarts. I'm always aware of my situation. I listen to my Spidey Senses.

And that day my Spidey Senses were freaking the fuck out.

It wasn't just the leering men on the sidewalk. It wasn't just the long, dark, empty halls I had to traverse every time I wanted to go to my room. It wasn't just the dimly lit room I stayed in. It wasn't just the fact that none of the hotel's exterior doors were locked. It wasn't just the fact that I couldn't see one camera or emergency call box in the garage. It wasn't just the creaky elevators that seemed to break down on the hour. It was *all* of it.

Looking back, I see that I ignored my Spidey Senses. They were going off like the fire alarm in the middle of my first night in the hotel. I know now that there were red flags *everywhere,* but really I should have checked into a different hotel immediately after a man stepped over me and swiped his balls across the top of my head. It was all downhill from there.

I should probably back up and explain that. So, I locked my car, got checked in, and went to my meeting downtown. And since I don't have valet kind of money, when I returned I needed to park my minivan in the garage.

It is kind of hard to imagine, but please try to envision my surprise when I found out the parking garage was even worse than the hotel. The only positive thing I can say about the place was that there were plenty of parking spaces. I found a spot and surveyed my over-stuffed minivan.

When I fly, I have a hard and fast rule that I can only pack two suitcases and two carry-ons otherwise I can't possibly carry everything in one trip to my rental car. But when I drive somewhere I always end up tossing more shit than I've ever needed into the car. I'll throw in an extra box of books, another bag of swag, a case of water, and a suitcase of nothing but shoes. I pack a banner and a tablecloth and 10,000 business cards just because I can. It feels like freedom.

And looking around the parking garage that day, I could see I wasn't the only lady author who thinks that way. All of the women around me were rolling in with a fuck ton of bags. Suitcases, boxes, totes, all of it. Many of them needed to use the rolling carts the hotel provided *for multiple trips*.

When I checked in I had been able to snag a coveted roller cart. Most everything I'd brought was being held for me in the lobby. I didn't have room on the cart for two roller bags, so I'd left them in my car thinking I could wrangle them up without a cart. But I'd forgotten I also had a box I needed to get inside. *Grr.*

I surveyed the situation and weighed the pros and cons. I hadn't seen my room yet, but I knew it was close to the elevators. I could see the bank of elevators from my parking spot, so I just needed to make it a few hundred feet and then I'd be on the home stretch. Because I'm a multi-tasking asshole who will carry eighty bags in one trip instead of making two trips, I piled everything together like two complicated Jenga games and slowly made my way toward the elevators.

The bags bounced over every divot in the concrete floor causing the box I'd perched on top to jostle precariously. I moved slowly and deliberately, praying the wheels on my overloaded bags didn't break. I looked up to check my progress and came face to face with the last obstacle that stood in my way: a glass door.

Yeah, there was a damn door between the parking garage and the elevators. It wasn't a security door where you needed a keycard or anything. It was just a stupid, useless door that you must hold open while you navigate everything you've packed through the smallest opening you can imagine.

"Great," I muttered.

I stood there for a full minute contemplating how I was going to manage the blasted door when I heard the elevator ding from the other side. The elevator doors slid open and revealed a man. He stepped off and pulled a ring of keys from his pants pocket.

Oh, good, I thought. *A hero has arrived. He can open the door for me.*

I waited expectantly for him to open the door but he just stopped and stared at me. For a good ten seconds we stood there, facing off. Me, with a stupid goofy smile that I hoped was friendly but not creepy and him with a deep scowl. I am slow to understand people's emotions, so it took me a bit to register that his scowl was intended for me and not for the world at large which is who my scowl is usually intended for. He was clearly irritated by my presence on the other side of that door. He was literally sneering at me. So I fumbled for the door thinking that would be an excellent physical clue for him to snap into action. Instead, he stood there and watched me.

Oh shit. He is not my hero. He is not going to help me at all. Oh, okay, fuck him. I am a strong, independent woman, hear me roar, motherfucker.

I wrenched open the door and started to guide the first bag through the doorway. As the suitcase bumped over the raised threshold, everything piled on top shifted and the suitcase toppled over, crashing to the floor and dumping the contents of my purse everywhere.

"Fuck," I muttered. I bent over to pick up the stuff, letting the door bang into my ass, and the dude continued to stand there! He made no effort to help me. It was hot as hell, I was tired, and I was ready to fight, I looked up and said, "Don't worry, I got it."

"Okay," he said, and then STEPPED OVER me and my belongings.

Let me repeat that. He. Stepped. Over. Me. He literally stepped over me. Only his legs weren't as long as he thought or I wasn't as short as he assumed, because his motherfucking junk brushed the top of my head!

When I felt his soft, flaccid package brush the top of my head I was so shocked I was speechless. He was about five or ten feet from me when I could finally speak again. I stood up and said, "Wow, what an asshole!"

He looked back and glared at me.

I stood straighter and glared right back. "Yeah, I'm talking to you. What the fuck is wrong with you? You're the rudest fucking person on the planet."

He just shrugged, got in his car, and drove off.

I didn't need him to hoist my suitcase onto his manly shoulders and carry it to my hotel room. All he had to do was be like, "Here, let me hold the door while you drag your bags through."

I swear, the older I get the less help I get. It's like I'm not young enough anymore to be cute and helpless but I'm not yet old enough to be frail. But it's a matter of common decency. If you see someone struggling with a door, *hold the fucking door, asshole!*

I FINALLY HAULED ALL my shit to my hotel room. (Spoiler alert: it took three trips. I should have just done three from the beginning. When will I ever learn?) I was exhausted and ready for bed. I tried to lock my door but discovered there wasn't a bolt and the extra security lock really didn't latch well. "Are you fucking kidding me?" I complained to myself, flipping the useless latch back and forth. "I'm so going to get murdered tonight."

I knew the hotel was sold out so changing rooms wasn't an option. I did the best I could: I put on my jammies and hunkered down for a long, sleepless night at the Bates Motel with fifty pounds of books stacked in front of the door. I was just starting to relax when there was a knock on my door.

I am too short to see through the peep hole, so I yelled, "Who's there?"

A woman said, "Housekeeping."

Hmm, I thought. I'd been warned at check-in not to open my door to any strangers. "Sometimes our...neighbors...bother our guests," the man at the desk said.

But it seemed legit. I shoved the boxes of books a couple of inches so I could carefully, cautiously crack open the door. A woman in a uniform stood in the hallway with a clipboard in her hand. "Yeah?" I asked.

She looked stunned to see me. "Oh! It looks like they put someone in here."

"Huh?" Of course they did. She'd answered my question earlier!

She consulted her clipboard. "I was told this room needed cleaning."

Are you fucking kidding me? If the murderers didn't get me, the goddamn bedbugs would!"Seriously?" I screeched. "This room hasn't been cleaned?"

"Was the room...clean...when you moved in?" she asked, peering over my head. I am not a neat person. When I move into a hotel room, *I move in*. I get comfortable, if you know what I mean. It looked like I'd exploded all over the room. Books and swag were stacked everywhere. I had a thousand devices strewn across the desk, charging. Makeup and clothes were scattered about. The bed was torn apart and a wet towel was draped over a chair. It was a disaster area.

"Was it clean?" I asked.

I thought that was a very subjective question. The hotel, in general, was a fucking cesspool. I didn't think it had been "clean" since 1980. Earlier I'd wiped down every surface in that room with a dozen Clorox wipes and I was fairly certain I heard billions of germs crying out in pain. The couch had so many mystery stains, I'd chosen to stand all evening instead of risk sitting on it. The carpet turned my socks black, so I busted out my "hotel flip flops" as soon as arrived. (Doesn't everyone pack a pair of flip flops to wear in the hotel because the carpet is probably gross? Just me?) I'd even worn my "hotel flip flops" in the shower, for goodness sake. That's how much I trusted the cleanliness of that room.

"I mean, the bed was made when I got here..." I said.

She nodded. "Oh, okay, then it's a mistake. It was cleaned."

She walked away and left me standing there questioning everything I'd ever known.

I wanted to scream, *BUT WAS IT CLEANED???*

My mind raced. I'd already used the towels I found hanging on the towel bar. Suddenly I couldn't remember if they'd been clean and fresh when they were hung neatly or if they'd been used and drip-drying? Bile rose in my throat. I'd already been in the bed. My head immediately started itching. I looked at the complimentary bottle of water I'd been chugging. Did I break the seal on that thing or did someone else? Before I could spiral, I called down to the front desk and waited on hold until a human finally answered. I asked to change rooms and was reminded the hotel was fully booked. "Fine," I sighed. "Please ask housekeeping to bring me new sheets and towels at least." No one ever showed up with my request.

I survived that night by thinking about my childhood. I've spent countless nights sleeping on the disgusting floors of many Motels 6 and 8 across the country. My brother and I played rock-paper-scissors to see who could "win" the prized, revolting, spooge-covered comforter to wrap up in. I figured if that didn't kill me, this wouldn't either.

In the morning I stripped the bed and threw all the sheets and towels on the floor. I left a nice tip and a note asking the housekeeping staff to please clean the room thoroughly. I can't be sure, but I think they put the same sheets back on my bed. Either that or ALL of the hotel's sheets have holes in the upper left-hand corner.

Ew.

I couldn't obsess over it anymore. I just had to let it go

and focus on the positive. Sure, the hotel was creepy and gross. Yes, my nerves were frayed from nightly fire alarms and announcements telling us to "shelter in place" due to "intruders in the building." You bet I was drinking insane amounts of alcohol to wash down the inedible food I was served. But I was having a great time at the event and I'd met a ton of nice people.

IT WAS the last day of the conference and I was feeling a lot better about my chances of dying in a normal, random way like being hit by a bus when an elevator almost fell out of the sky and reminded me the hotel was constantly trying to murder me.

That afternoon, I couldn't handle another mystery meat sandwich, so I'd joined some friends for lunch at a nearby restaurant. When we returned to the hotel there were a dozen fire trucks and ambulances lined up along the curb with their lights flashing.

"Hey, you ladies be careful," the Uber driver said. "This neighborhood isn't safe."

Yeah, we know, dude.

We side-stepped busy first responders and entered the packed lobby. I asked a woman near the door, "What's going on?"

"It's crazy," she said. "An elevator is stuck between floors. It's full of people. It's been up there for a long time."

Shit! There were only three elevators in the whole place. One was already broken when we arrived. (Because of course it was.) And now one had authors and readers trapped inside, high above the lobby. Luckily the hot firemen were there to rescue them. There was only one elevator left running and I wasn't crazy about hopping on it.

The whole afternoon was supposed to be a book-signing, so we'd left our books and swag in the ballroom on the top floor, but that's where the other elevator was stuck.

I calculated my losses. I'd checked out earlier that day and almost everything was already packed in my car. I had my purse, my phone, and my keys with me. I contemplated jumping in my car and noping the fuck outta there. But I'd worked so hard that weekend and all my earnings were up there. Besides my cash box, I had hundreds of dollars of inventory in the room too. Plus, my favorite Vera Bradley tote bag. If we're being honest, I really went back for Vera. And my cash. But mostly Vera.

I waited patiently for my turn to trap myself in a metal box of death. I held my breath all the way up and arrived unscathed. The woman signing books beside me filled me in on Elevator: The Horror Movie. She said she'd been eating lunch in the open atrium a couple of floors below us when the elevator broke and it was terrifying to see. In the atrium the elevators are visible through a glass enclosure and she heard a loud noise and could see the cables swinging wildly and banging around against the glass.

"That's when the elevator made a horrific noise and lurched a bit. But then everything stopped."

"Oh my god," I said.

"I know! I was just waiting for the elevator to fall in front of my eyes," she said, shuddering.

"But it didn't fall," I said.

"Not yet," she said, ominously.

Fucking hell.

The elevator's near disaster put a bit of a damper on the rest of the afternoon's mood. We got news that everyone had been rescued but that the elevators were going to be used on a limited basis.

I was told, "Please use the stairs if you are able."

I was more than happy to take the stairs! Nothing motivated me to slash prices more than the idea of carrying fifty pounds of books down fifteen flights of stairs.

In the end, despite the shitastic hotel experience, I had a great time at the conference. I met so many lovely people. And I did not get murdered. Nor did an elevator plummet to the basement. However, I did find out that there is a very nice hotel just a few blocks over and if I ever go back to this conference again, that is where I will stay next time!

SIXTEEN

WHY YOU SHOULD ALWAYS PACK AN UMBRELLA

NEW YORK CITY

2019

I was hired to record the audiobook for *People I Want to Punch in the Throat*, but I had to do it in New York City. I picked a long weekend so we could go a few days early and bring the kids. In the past when we went to New York City, I always had to work while the Hubs and kids got to have fun without me. This time I wanted to join them when they went to eat pizza, and Chinese food, and more pizza, and desserts as big as their heads. I wanted to visit the Hubs' mom with them. I wanted to go sightseeing, and shopping, and eat one more pizza pie with them before I had to go to work.

It had been a few years since I'd taken my kids to New York City and it was their first time visiting as "big kids." Basically, they were all grown up on this trip. The kids were taller than me and could see better over the crowds. Their legs were longer than mine and I had a hard time keeping up with them. They had GPS on their cell phones, so they didn't need anyone telling them where to go. We didn't have to hold their hands and make sure they were right beside us at all times. They could cross the street by themselves and they enjoyed going down to the corner by our hotel to get another slice of pizza on their own after we ate pizza for dinner. (What can I say? We have terrible pizza in Kansas, so we try to load up when we're in New York.)

The kids were so grown up that Adolpha had her first experience with a pervert and her first experience with the village of women who protect one another from asshole men.

WE'D SPENT A LONG, cold, dreary day out at Liberty Island. (Yes, I dragged my family to tour the Statue of Liberty like typical Midwestern tourists. Because that's what we are! Can you believe that even though the Hubs lived in New York City for almost twenty-five years he'd never been? I wasn't going to let that happen to my kids!) We were tired and soggy and had a lengthy subway ride back to our hotel in midtown waiting for us. By the time everyone peed, bought a souvenir, had a snack (probably pizza), and took one last selfie with Lady Liberty we found ourselves trying to catch the subway during rush hour. The trains were packed tightly with exhausted, irritable, drenched commuters. The other tourists had the brains to avoid the subway at rush hour or the budget to pay for an Uber back to the hotel. The Hubs was never going to spring for an Uber, so I steeled myself, awakened my long-dormant inner New Yorker, and pushed my way through the throng to get onto the train carriage. We ended up separated (not holding hands will do that to a group). Adolpha and I found a space to stand near one another at one end of the train car and the Hubs and Gomer were together at the other.

At each stop, more people pressed on, jostling us, and I reminded Adolpha again where to get off in case we became separated. When we arrived at a busy station, many people jumped up to exit the train. I nudged Adolpha toward two newly vacant seats together along the bench running the length of the car. We moved quickly and grabbed them. My feet were tired, so I slid in gratefully next to a middle-aged woman who appeared to be sleeping. I barely noticed her, because it is not an uncommon sight to see people napping on the subway. She was curled away from me toward a partition that flanked the automatic doors.

When I moved to New York City in the 1990s as a fresh-faced Midwesterner I learned very quickly that smiling and making contact with my fellow commuters was not appropriate subway etiquette. In fact, it might get you punched in the throat. More than once I was asked, "The fuck you looking at?" or told, "Keep your eyes to your fucking self, you fucking weirdo." I was cured of my over-friendliness within my first few weeks of commuting when a man standing directly in front of me asked, "How are you today?" I looked up from my seat prepared to have a friendly conversation about my day only to be greeted by his penis poking through his unzipped fly and wagging in my face. When I screamed and swatted at him to move, the man next to me looked over the top of his newspaper and asked me, "Well, what did you think he wanted?"

Ever since those days, if I ride the subway without a book to read, my eyes are either planted firmly on the floor or gazing off into space. I keep my face downright hostile but the Spidey Senses that women have, always on high alert, push out and taste the air, reading the environment without my dumb face grinning at everyone.

The doors next to the sleeping woman opened and almost everyone on the platform waited for the dozens of people to exit. Except one large man. My senses starting tingling when he angrily and loudly pushed through the masses and claimed a space in the doorway, his body leaning against the partition where the sleeping woman dozed against the other side. As people entered the car, he was directly in the way, but he pushed and shoved and was belligerent toward anyone who touched him. No one confronted him, though. He was bigger than everyone around and no one wanted to take him on. They just wanted to get home. Once everyone was on and the doors shut again, he spread his body even wider pressing against the partition. He was so tall that his ass butted up against the sleeping woman's head. When the train lurched forward, he stumbled a bit and accidentally (or maybe on purpose) bumped against her head.

She woke up in a fury and poked him, hard. "Get the fuck back," she snarled. Passengers don't get much personal space on a crowded subway train during rush hour, but he was clearly stepping over her line. He moved a fraction of an inch away from her, grumbling about her under his breath. She refused to back down and continued to glare at him all while fixing her hair.

He unleashed a slew of names and I watched as she glared at him one last time before she shut her eyes again. He didn't take his eyes off her and I could feel his rage building. I watched him carefully, wondering what I'd do if this fight went further. Would I jump to her defense? I only had a few more stops to go, maybe I could ignore them and hope the train moved faster? My daughter was right beside me. The last time we took the kids to New York City they witnessed a brutal attack on a homeless man and were still traumatized by it. I didn't want Adolpha to get sideways in a fight I didn't have a dog in. But on the other hand, what kind of person would sit there and watch a giant man berate a woman? Not me. So I decided. I'd have to jump in. I was the closest woman to her. We were surrounded by men, oblivious (and uninterested) on their phones, earbuds jammed tightly in their ears. In all my years of living in New York City and witnessing shitty behavior on subways, I'd learned it was only the women you could rely on for help. I only ever saw women helping women.

I imagined screaming at him, kicking him in the balls, and, of course, punching him in the throat. I didn't have mace in my bag but I could bash him with Adolpha's hefty Hydroflask I was carrying for her. I girded my loins. I was ready.

But before I had to fight the dude, the train arrived at our stop.

"This is us," I told Adolpha, a wave of relief washing over me.

I hopped up from the seat and pulled her close to me. My kids are true Midwesterners who say "Ope" and ask to "Squeeze by," so when we're in New York City, the Hubs and I tend take the lead so we can carve a path for our children a la mama duck style. I plowed through the Land of Manspread with Adolpha hot on my heels. "Stay close," I muttered. Getting on and off a crowded subway train were the only times on that trip I felt the overwhelming urge to grab her hand. My kids are like veal and even though we'd made a plan if the train doors closed before they could exit, I wasn't sure what they'd really do in that moment of panic.

Luckily, we managed to get off the train without incident and hopped on the escalator behind the Hubs and Gomer and I breathed a sigh of relief. That's when the sleeping woman from the train tapped me on the shoulder. She was riding behind me. "Ma'am, you need to be careful with your daughter," she said, nodding at Adolpha.

"What do you mean?" I asked. I looked at Adolpha and I was shocked to see she looked a little ashamed.

"It's okay," the woman said kindly to Adolpha. She motioned behind her. "That big guy on the train. You noticed him, right?"

I nodded, "The one who bumped you? Of course I did."

"Yeah, he was trying to grab her butt."

"What?" I screeched. "She's 12 years old!"

She shrugged. "He don't care. He still tried to grab it."

"Her 12-YEAR-OLD BUTT? Where is he?" I scanned the platform below, hoping to catch a glimpse of him. Forget beaning him with a Hydroflask, I was ready to shove his head up his ass. He touched my daughter's butt. Her butt!!

"He stayed on the train," Adolpha said quietly.

The woman nodded. "Yeah, when you were getting off the train, you had her behind you and he was behind her, like, cupping her butt. You couldn't see him. But I did. That's when I hit him with my umbrella." She rattled the black umbrella in her hand like it was a sword.

"You hit him?" I asked. I was awestruck. I mean, I talk a big talk when it comes to punching people in the throat, but at the end of the day I'm mostly bark and very little bite. I could have told him off and made him cry for his mommy, but *hitting* him was something else. I've said it before and I'll say it again: That guy was big. Bigger than the average man. He was mean and angry. Hitting him with an umbrella was the equivalent of poking an actual bear. I was impressed by her courage. And grateful.

Adolpha nodded. "She did, Mom. I didn't know what was happening. He was so close to me. I elbowed him like you taught me, but he wouldn't move. He just got closer. He wouldn't stop grabbing at me. He was trying to get under my raincoat, but he couldn't figure it out. But no matter what I did, he wouldn't back off or stop. Not until she hit him." Adolpha still looked guilty and it broke my heart. I could see the woman was upset too. I knew that we both were thinking back to the first time a man put his hands on us without permission. How angry, scared, and dirty we felt. And how guilty we felt, even though we did nothing wrong. Fuck! I wanted to scream. I didn't want my 12-year-old daughter to already be dealing with this shit.

"I don't usually get involved, but lately...as I get older..." she trailed off. "I don't know, he was bugging me before and then when I saw him do that to her, I had to stop him, you know?"

I nodded, sadly. I knew what she meant. Back in my twenties I would have never hit a man on the subway for groping a girl, but now in my forties I'd beat that mother-fucker with another motherfucker.

She said sternly, "But you need to put her in front of you, men are assholes."

"They sure are," I said. "Listen, thank you so much. I'm so glad you were there. And I'm so glad you told me this." Because I had a sneaking suspicion Adolpha would not have told me right away.

The woman smiled. "I wasn't sure if I should tell you. Some moms don't like to be told, but I just thought you should know. She wasn't doing anything...you know...to encourage him...she was just standing there and he was right up against her."

I wanted to scream, *Of course she was!! I want to hunt his ass down! I want his balls on a platter! I want to shame him so hard his mother calls and apologizes for his behavior!* But instead I said, "I believe you."

She nodded. "Good. Because I could tell she was young and had no idea what to do."

"She knows what to do, but sometimes everyone needs some help," I said. "I'm so glad you—and your umbrella—were there. Thank you."

She shook her umbrella again. "Of course! We gotta look out for the girls. That's what we do, right?"

We'd reached the top of the escalator and went our separate ways with a nod.

That night I talked to Adolpha about staying in front of me and always making a scene if someone gets too close to her. "A good man, a nice man, will always move if you ask him to," I said. "When you ask him to move, he moves and shows you he's a good guy. It's the bad ones who argue with you or try to convince you they're good. I can't protect you from all the bad men out there. And the good men are either oblivious or disinterested in helping."

I frowned, thinking about the Hubs and Gomer. They're good men, but they're blind as hell and still need to do some major changing. When I told the Hubs what had transpired on the subway, his first comment was, "Well, she *is* wearing yoga pants."

OH, HELL NO!

I don't care if she was naked, that doesn't give anyone the right to lay hands on her body. For years, women like me and the lady from the train have put up with that kind of shit and we're exhausted. In the last few years more and more women are speaking out about the abuse they've endured. I don't know one woman my age who hasn't been groped, kissed, grabbed, or assaulted by a man. Not one. My earliest memory of such abuse was my freshman year of high school when boys kept snapping my bra strap. I was mortified and embarrassed by my body and I did my best to cover it up, hoping they'd leave me alone, but they wouldn't stop. Finally, I fought back and won, but I was sent to the principal's office. The principal sat across the desk from me surveying me coldly and said, "You have to understand, Jenni. Boys have certain biological urges and you girls and the way you dress, you're not helping them one bit." I was wearing a XXL sweatshirt. There was nothing enticing about my outfit.

I didn't have the words to express it then, but I do now. It wasn't about their desire for me; it was about their disgust for me. They wanted to hold power over me, to show me they were better than me, and that I could be broken. It took me decades to build my self-esteem back up after years of that kind of shit—and I'm one of the lucky ones. The fuck I was going to let my daughter go down the same path because her dad spouts idiotic nonsense.

"She's wearing yoga pants under a giant sweater and a raincoat. You can't even see her butt," I replied, angrily. "She did nothing wrong."

Since then Adolpha has learned how to throw her elbow harder. She's learned how to yell, "Quit touching my ass, you pervert!" And she learned that when she's in trouble, look to the women, because most women will have your back.

"Especially the middle-aged ones," I said. "We've all had our asses groped on the subway and we're fucking tired of it and if we can stop another generation of girls from getting groped, we will!"

I will always be grateful to the sleeping woman on the train, because she taught me it takes a motherfucking village to protect ourselves and all the young girls in our care. Luckily it was raining that day and the sleeping woman had an umbrella, but I've decided I'm going to always pack an umbrella so I can carry one even on sunny days because I would love to beat a motherfucker with my umbrella.

SEVENTEEN

I'M STILL NOT CONVINCED I DIDN'T HALLUCINATE THIS ENCOUNTER

LAS VEGAS, NEVADA

2020

I am a magnet for weirdness. I have always been a magnet for weirdness. It seems like I can't leave my house without a bizarre or strange encounter. Sometimes people will write to me and accuse me of lying about or embellishing the abnormal situations I find myself in. I get a little offended because my imagination isn't that great. But really, honestly, sometimes even I'm surprised by situations I encounter. I find myself looking over my shoulder for a hidden camera.

One of those incidents happened in the Las Vegas airport. I know the slogan, "What happens in Vegas, stays in Vegas," but come on, I don't keep anything a secret.

I was sitting in my gate area very early one morning waiting for my 7:30 flight. Completely alone in that deserted airport, I realized no one leaves Vegas at the ass-crack of dawn. Apparently, they were all back in their hotel rooms sleeping off their hangovers or mourning their gambling losses or stumbling in from a long night on the town.

It wasn't surprising how empty the airport was, but it was a bit unnerving. Normally when I fly through

McCarran International Airport it's so stuffed with people I can't find a seat. I've spent more time sitting on the floor of that airport than in a chair. It was so empty I was just beginning to wonder if The Rapture had happened and I'd been left behind when I saw a woman stumbling down the long desolate hallway toward me.

I am not a gambler. When I travel to Las Vegas I spend my money on shopping and spas. And when I run out of money I spend time people watching. I love to see the unique outfits and hair styles that seem to only exist in Vegas. I love to eavesdrop on people's stories and speculate about what brought them to Sin City. Over my many visits to Las Vegas, I've seen some incredibly interesting people, but I did a double-take when I saw the woman lurching toward me. She had a whole thing going on and it was a lot to behold.

Imagine a short, white, rotund woman in flesh-colored leggings. She wore a tightly fitting t-shirt that was so long it could have passed for a dress. As she stumbled toward me, the shirt hitched higher and higher up her hips, revealing her body. I couldn't tell if I was glimpsing her actual skin or the (white) skin-colored leggings, but either way it wasn't a good look. The t-shirt slash dress had a cartoon image of an enormous Tweety Bird emblazoned across the front. She was either bra-less or her bra was broken, because her boobies were hanging low and swinging in opposite directions. Her feet were stuffed into enormous furry boots that practically came up to her knees. (It was February, but the weather wasn't cold enough for such boots.) Her hair was half gray and half blond, one side matted completely against her head while the other side looked like she had been electrocuted. In one hand she carried four or five plastic grocery sacks that I could see were overflowing with clothes, charging cords, and another pair of furry boots. In her other hand she carried a cell phone. She was having a conversation on speakerphone.

Normally I get very irritated when people have conversations on speakerphone, but this time I was actually quite excited. I could tell this was going to be a doozy of a conversation and I didn't want to miss one word. As she got closer, I could hear her wheezing loudly.

"Hang on," she said in a thick southern Missouri twang. "I gotta sit down. I'm dying." She stopped and sat down heavily one seat away from me.

One. Seat. Away. From. Me.

My entire gate area and the one next to it were completely empty. I was literally the only person around and she sat down one seat away from me. I was either going to be mugged or I was going to have the best story ever—maybe both.

I pulled out my laptop and opened a new document. I pretended I was working but really I was listening intently and transcribing her whole conversation. I called it "The Adventures of Furry Boots."

"Are you on the plane?" the woman on the other end of the phone asked.

"No, you're not listenin'," Furry Boots growled. "I told you what happened already!"

Besides the twang, I could detect some kind of speech impediment. Maybe a lisp or something? I couldn't tell exactly.

"I *am* listening!" the other woman argued. "You're the one who's not making any damn sense!"

"All right, all right. I'm gonna tell you one more time, so open your ears and listen to me! I'm gonna be getting in late. I missed the damn flight. I got another one, but it doesn't leave yet and I gotta connect somewhere first before I get to Branson."

Branson! I thought, patting myself on the back for guessing her accent correctly. *I knew that accent was Ozarky!*

"But why did you miss the flight?" the friend asked.

Fuzzy Boots sighed. "That's what I'm trying to tell ya! I was s'posed to fly to Branson this morning."

"I know that part!" the woman snapped.

"But the airlines said if I didn't want to miss the flight, I needed to be at the airport at four o'clock."

"That's ridiculous!"

"Well, I don't know about that, 'cause I missed the fucking flight, now didn't I?" Furry Boots exclaimed.

The friend sighed. "Fuck yeah, you did."

"Anyway, I got to thinking yesterday morning. If I have to be at the airport at four in the fucking morning, why should I pay for a night in the hotel?" Furry Boots reasoned.

"Damn right," the friend agreed.

Was this real? I wondered. *Who thinks like this? Did I stumble into some crazy reality show or something?*

I looked around for a hidden cameraperson, but we were alone.

Furry Boots kept going. "So I called the front desk and told them I was checking out a day early. And they was like, 'Okay, bye.' But then they kicked me out of my room."

"Why would they do that?"

"I don't know 'cause check-out is noon, or something. All I know is they knocked on my door and told me to get the fuck out. So I had to grab my shit and go. But I left my suitcase!"

"What?" The friend was confused. "How did you leave your suitcase?"

Right? I'm with you, friend. How it the hell does someone leave their suitcase in a hotel room?

"I don't know. I got so fucking confused. Probably because I was drunk. And I felt rushed! There was a dude telling me to hurry up or they'd charge me for another day. So I shoved everything in grocery sacks."

The woman on the phone laughed. "So you don't got any suitcase?"

"No! But it don't matter. That part's not important!"

I don't know, Furry Boots. I think it sounds a bit important. But, go on. We're all listening.

"I got my shit in the bags and I go to the casino. Because I figured I'm gonna take that money I saved on the hotel room and gamble till it's time to go to the airport."

"Yeah, what the fuck else can you do?"

"Right? It's Vegas. That's what I'm fucking here for. So I find myself a slot machine and I go to *work*, you know what I'm saying?"

"Hell yeah, I do. It *is* work! Double that money!"

"Exactly. The waitress keeps bringing me drinks and I just keep fucking drinking, because why not? I'm losing, though. Fucking slots," Furry Boots spat.

"You should have played poker. You're good at poker."

"The poker here is different," Furry Boots explained.

"Oh, I didn't know that."

Up until that point I'd been doing a pretty good job keeping my facial expression somewhere between neutral and bored. But I couldn't stop myself from giving her a side-eye. *I'm being duped, right?* I thought. *Or I'm asleep and dreaming all of this.*

"So, I'm down real fast. I got no money for food. I held back cab fare for the airport. But I gotta keep going. Change my luck, right? I ask the waitress if I can have some pretzels or something. Anything, because I'm drunk as fuck, you know?"

"Anybody would be drunk as fuck if they didn't give you no food with your alcohol."

"That's what I'm sayin'! The waitress was like, 'The buffet is good.'"

"The buffet? Like you got money for that!"

"She's a goddamn moron. So I just keep drinking and gambling—"

"Losing."

"Shut the fuck up," Furry Boots snapped. "My luck turned, bitch. I'm there all day losing and all of a sudden I'm almost out of money and I start winning."

"You did not!"

"I did! I was winning like a motherfucker!"

"Holy shit. That's amazing!"

"Yeah, but that's when the casino bosses got mad at me," Furry Boots said.

"What do you mean they got mad?"

"I was winning *too* much. They needed to stop me."

I practically snorted, but I managed to make it look like a cough. "Excuse me," I said when Furry Boots glared at me. "All the cigarette smoke triggers my allergies."

Furry Boots gave me a curt nod and exclaimed, "That's when they told the waitress to put something in my drink."

The friend gasped. "Are you shitting me? They drugged you?"

"Fuck yeah, they did!"

"How do you know?"

"Because the last time I looked at my clock I had about two hours 'til I had to leave for the airport. I was up big. *Real big!* And then, boom!" Furry Boots yelled.

Her friend was hooked. "Boom?! What happened?"

I stopped pretending at this point. I was fully invested in the story now. I needed to know what happened, too. I practically leaned over the empty seat between us so I wouldn't miss a word.

Furry Boots shrugged. "I don't know, exactly. One minute I've got hours to go and I'm winnin' and the next minute I wake up on the floor of the casino with two security guards kicking me in my fucking ass."

I wish I had popcorn, I thought wistfully. *This story deserves popcorn.*

"You did not!"

"I did too! They was kicking me and telling me to get the fuck out. They said I got drunk and I been passed out for two hours!" Furry Boots was indignant.

"Passed out on the floor for two hours! What? Nobody helped you or nothing?"

"I don't believe 'em. I did not do that. I've never passed out in my life."

I could almost hear the friend nodding vigorously. "You can hold your liquor."

"Exactly," Furry Boots agreed. "So, I was like, 'Where's my money?' and they was like, 'What money, bitch? You broke.'"

"No way! They stole your money!"

"Yes! All the money I won was gone. The casino stole it back! They didn't like that I was winning so much!" Furry Boots raged.

"Oh my god! They were out to get you from the minute they kicked you out of your hotel room!"

"And then I look around for my shit and half of it's gone," Furry Boots wailed.

I counted her bags. She still had five sacks. How many did she start with? Also, who carries around that many plastic sacks just in case they get too drunk and forget their suitcase? The holes in Furry Boots story were starting to get bigger. *We must be reaching the big reveal part of the show,* I thought. I dug around in my bag for my lipstick. I didn't want to look so washed out when the host appeared to ask me "What were you thinking, Jen, as you listened to this outrageous story?"

"Gone? It got stolen, too?"

"Yes! All I got left is, like, some dirty underwear and a pair of boots. That dress I borrowed is gone."

The friend's voice raised an octave. "*My* dress? *My* dress got stolen?"

"Yup. It's gone. Sorry 'bout that," Furry Boots said, but when she rolled her eyes at me, she did not look sorry.

I stifled a laugh.

"Fuck!"

"But that's not the worst part," Furry Boots said.

"There's more?"

"I sit up and I get my shit together and I feel weird."

"Well, yeah, you got drugged!"

"No, it was something else. Like, I can't explain it, but something's different. And then it hits me: my teeth are gone!"

Only she pronounced the word "teeth" like "teef."

This is the point where I was finally brave enough to stand up and pretend I needed to stretch. But really I wanted to see Furry Boots mouth. I bent over to touch my toes and when I came up, Furry Boots was grinning at me. Sure enough, her two front teeth were missing. That explained the speech impediment I'd noticed earlier.

"Your teeth?? The new ones you just got?"

Furry Boots nodded. "Yep! They're gone! I couldn't find them anywhere!"

"Damn! So, what, you got no teeth now?"

"No! The security guards want me to go, but I'm on the floor looking for my teeth—"

Her friend gasped. "You don't think they was stolen too?" she wondered.

"I don't think so. They was good teeth, but I don't think they'd be good for anyone but me. I think they got knocked out when I fell off the chair—"

"Because of the drugs," the friend interjected.

"Right. But I can't find them anywhere. And while I'm searching I notice the time."

"Oh, shit."

"Yep. I'm way late at that point. So I'm like, fuck the teeth. I gotta go. I grab a cab and I give him all the money I can find. I'm throwing like change and shit at him."

"It's still money," the friend said helpfully.

"I get in the airport and I hear them announcing my flight. It's going without me."

"Oh no," the friend said, realization dawning upon her.

"Yeah, I gotta run. And you know I can't run with the asthma," Furry Boots said matter-of-factly.

"You've always had trouble with running. Even before you got the asthma."

"So, I'm trying, but it's not working. And I gotta get through security still. But I think security will be fast, because I left all my shampoo and shit at the hotel. I got nothing—"

"Except some dirty underwear and a pair of boots."

"Right. So I throw my shit on that conveyor belt thing and I try to go through the metal detector but I forgot to take off my boots and the policeman goes fuckin' wild."

"No!"

"Yes! He's like, 'Ma'am! You need to remove your shoes'

or whatever. I said, 'I don't have time for this shit. My plane is leaving!'"

"Right? Like you're gonna hide a bomb in your boots!"

"He says all mean, 'Take off your boots!' So I take 'em off and guess what falls out of my boot?"

"What?"

"My hunting knife."

"Oh, shit," the friend whispered.

Oh, shit, indeed, I thought. I was back to my initial assessment that this story might end with my murder.

Furry Boots exhaled loudly. "Yep. I told the policeman, 'I totally forgot I had a knife in my boot.' And he says, 'Why do you have a knife in your boot?'"

"Like it's crazy or something," the friend said.

Um, yeah, it is, I thought. *Super crazy.*

"And I says, 'Cause you don't spend all night gambling in a casino *without* a knife in your boot!'"

"Ain't that the fuckin' truth."

Furry Boots and I nodded wisely. I mean, she wasn't wrong.

"They take me in a room and I gotta talk to all kinds of people. I told them the casino drugged me but they didn't give a shit about that. All they cared about was the damn knife in my boot."

"The police in that town protect the casinos. They know who pays their bills," the friend said.

Furry Boots shuddered. "Then they let a lady policeman touch me to make sure I don't got no more contraband on me."

"Ugh. She probably liked it."

"Right? But they didn't find nothing else."

"Of course not! You only carry the one knife."

"Well, not no more. They kept the knife."

"They did?"

"Yep. Said I couldn't get it back."

"That's some bullshit right there. That was your daddy's knife!"

"It was a good fuckin' knife," Furry Boots said, bitterly.

"So that's why you missed the plane."

"Yep."

"All right. Well, I guess we'll see you when we see you."

Furry Boots hung up the phone and looked around, a bit dazed. She turned in her chair and asked me, "Where the fuck is everybody?"

I was speechless, so I kind of shrugged because what do you say to someone after a story like that?

"You're going to Branson, right?"

"No, I'm going to Chicago," I replied.

"Ah, fuck," Furry Boots said. "I'm in the wrong goddamn place again." She gathered her sacks of dirty underwear and boots. She dialed her phone.

"Hello?" I recognized the friend's voice.

"Girl, you're never going to believe this. I think I missed the fucking plane again. Fuck this, I'm going back to the casino."

I wanted to say, "But you don't have your knife in your boot!"

THANK YOU!

Thank you for reading this book! I appreciate your support and I hope you enjoyed it. I also hope you will tell a friend— or 30 about this book!

Would you please do me a huge favor and leave me a review anywhere you leave book reviews? Of course I prefer 5-star, but I'll take what I can get.

- Jen

ABOUT THE AUTHOR

Jen Mann is best known for her wildly popular and hysterical blog People I Want to Punch in the Throat. She has been described by many as Erma Bombeck—with f-bombs. Jen is known for her hilarious rants and funny observations on everything from parenting to gift giving to celebrity behavior to politics to Elves on Shelves. She does not suffer fools lightly. Jen is the author of the *New York Times* bestseller *People I Want to Punch in the Throat: Competitive Crafters, Drop-Off Despots, and Other Suburban Scourges* which was a Finalist for a Goodreads Reader's Choice Award. Her latest book is *How I F*cking Did It: From Moving Elves to Making Over Six-Figures on the Internet and You Can Too*. She is also the mastermind behind the *New York Times* bestselling *I Just Want to Pee Alone* series.

facebook.com/jen.mann.568

twitter.com/throat_punch

instagram.com/jenmannauthor

Made in the USA
Monee, IL
09 July 2021